Mimi Khalvati was born in Iran, grew up on the Isle of Wight and attended Drama Centre London. Her Carcanet collections include *In White Ink* (1991), *Mirrorwork* (1995), for which she received an Arts Council of England Writer's Award, and *Entries on Light* (1997). Her *Selected Poems* was published by Carcanet in 2000. She was poet in residence at the Royal Mail as part of The Poetry Society's Poetry Places scheme and is Coordinator of The Poetry School.

Pascale Petit was born in Paris, grew up in France and Wales and has an MA in sculpture from the Royal College of Art. She is a Poetry School tutor and poetry editor of *Poetry London*. Her first full-length collection, *Heart of a Deer*, was published by Enitharmon in 1998. She has twice travelled to the Venezuelan Amazon and is currently completing her second collection, *The Zoo Father*. She was shortlisted for the Forward Best Single Poem prize in 2000.

TYING THE SONG

a first anthology from The Poetry School
1997–2000

Edited by

Mimi Khalvati and Pascale Petit

London
ENITHARMON PRESS
2000

First published in 2000
by the Enitharmon Press
36 St George's Avenue
London N7 0HD

Distributed in Europe
by Littlehampton Book Services
through Signature Book Representation
2 Little Peter Street
Manchester M15 4PS

Distributed in the USA and Canada
by Dufour Editions Inc.
PO Box 7, Chester Springs
PA 19425, USA

ISBN 1 900564 76 9

British Library Cataloguing-in-Publication Data.
A catalogue record for this book is available
from the British Library.

The Enitharmon Press gratefully acknowledges a grant from the
London Arts Board towards the production costs of this volume.

Set in Bembo by Bryan Williamson, Frome,
and printed in Great Britain by
Biddles of Guildford

In memory of Blair Gibb

'After a while he goes to the word-passer, constantly humming the tune, and the word-passer, catching the air, joins in, and then sets a single word to it. This is called "tying the song", so that it may not "drift away" like an unmoored canoe.'

Kwakiutl, *Technicians of the Sacred*

Contents

Introduction

This book is a first for the School, a first for us as editors, and a first for some of our eleven poets. A few have already published collections, many have established an exciting track record in magazines, acquiring reputations as poets to watch for, and all of them we trust will go on to fulfil their promise. In each case, they are well on the way to first or new collections, have developed a distinctive voice and are committed to an ongoing journey in their work. Despite our epigraph, none of them are 'unmoored canoes' but in tying them together we hope to offer them safe harbour and a sparkling place to look back to once they are launched.

The Poetry School is entering its fourth year and this anthology is the first of a biennial series that will showcase the work of poets who have come through its doors. All of our contributors have attended courses or workshops, some from day one and still going strong, and each has entered warmly into the feeling of family that pervades the School. *Tying the Song* is dedicated to Blair Gibb, a Trustee and a moving spirit, who died tragically and is much mourned.

Common to our poets is a generous and affirming view of life, a vivid palette of expression and a wholehearted embrace of the value poetry has in their lives. This is not to say that they neglect the importance of technique and craft or that they are merely exponents of the much-derided 'workshop poem'. Rather, each has a vision that informs their body of work, and an idea of how they as individuals are looking to become part of the community of poets past and present. And that individuality is marked here by an unusual range of voice, tone and style.

This diversity reflects that of the School itself. What is The Poetry School? Where are you? we are often asked. Nowhere and everywhere, is the answer: we run workshops, courses, events at existing London venues – The Voice Box, The Poetry Society, the Barbican, Torriano Meeting House, and this year we are delighted to have a new home at Somerset House and the Courtauld Institute. Our courses range from reading courses that serve as introduction to world classics, to versification classes and cross-arts projects. In addition to our core programme, Special Events offer opportunities to work with visiting poets such as Marilyn Hacker, Les Murray, Charles Simic and C. K. Williams.

Having sprung from Saturday workshops run by Jane Duran and ourselves, and with the support of London Arts Board, we have grown in response to student demand into an open resource for poets at all stages of development, with over 500 enrolments a year. It is heartwarming to come across so much new talent – some of which will appear in future anthologies – and to find so many new poetry readers. All our tutors are established practitioners and every year new staff bring fresh perspectives to the School.

The work in this anthology was selected from submissions invited by tutors. Unlike most anthologies of new voices, ours includes many poems familiar to us – sometimes in successive drafts – and a few welcome discoveries. There are poems in free verse and traditional forms from those experienced in working with metre and rhyme and from others new to it and relishing the challenge. Longer poems, sequences and, in one case, cantos from a book-length poem in terza rima, counter the current vogue for page-length poems by offering, along with briefer pleasures, something more meaty for the avid reader.

The poets have also provided a short preface to place their poems in the wider context of their aspirations, ideas and experience. We met up with them all one Sunday in our Walthamstow office and asked them to choose a particular focus so that, taken together, their prefaces would give a composite picture of the writing process. In a couple of cases we taped informal chats with them. We hope these short pieces, along with the poems that encapsulate their own worlds, will invite the reader into further dialogues exploring some of the world poets are engaged with today.

MIMI KHALVATI & PASCALE PETIT

GRETA STODDART

Greta Stoddart writes:

A friend of mine recalls sitting through Tarkovsky's *Stalker* thinking it the most tedious film he'd ever seen. That night he tried to sleep but couldn't. The images of the film kept coming back to him, so much so that he had to get up and pace the room, he had to return to the film, he had to *think*. I recently saw *The Sound of Music* (again) and wept (again) when the Mother Superior sings 'Climb Every Mountain'. I'll forget about it till the next time it comes on when, no doubt, the nun and I will repeat our performances.

Rather than advocate tedious poetry I'd like to use this comparison to suggest that the emotions a poem provokes are not necessarily indicative of the memorability and, ultimately, the power of the poem. For some readers, the goosebump factor is paramount. The test of a worthwhile poem is based on their emotional response of which the 'tingle' factor is the single most satisfying symptom. Don't get me wrong. I like goose-bumps as much as the next person. But it's an automatic response, like a rush of adrenalin. Much as I enjoy reading these poems while they last, I rarely revisit them.

After reading certain writers you get the feeling your mind has altered, shifted in a way both minute and profound. We talk about seeing the world 'in a new light'. The greatest poets have this ability to transform 'real life' or, as in the case of Elizabeth Bishop, make 'things as they are seem to be even more themselves once she has written them'.* Not all of this has to do with emotion. It has also perhaps to do with a supreme observance, a kind of revelation at once startling and true.

Naturally, as a writer, your initial impulse needs to be emotional to some degree. But the poem itself, especially if it's been dragged kicking and screaming into the world, ought finally to come to some kind of resolve that it will, if it's any good, have thoroughly earned.

You hear of poets claiming to be unable to recite a poem because it's too 'painful'. To be literally 'choked with emotion' may be a painful state, and one that must be got through, but it is ultimately a fruitless one and one that will rarely lead to the writing of a half-decent poem. Aspiring to something beyond the twanging of heartstrings, 'stepping out of ourselves', is to step onto a path that will lead us to a new kind of awareness.

---

* 'Counting to a Hundred: On Elizabeth Bishop', Seamus Heaney, *The Redress of Poetry* (London: Faber, 1990)

The Fitter

It can take days. *The vision, you see, is vital,*
without it, it's nothing – a soft toy. Pass me
my eyes, pointing to an old biscuit tin.

It's a kind of hunting all over again, with books
open, photos pinned, ready with needle
and glue. They caught the body years ago,
that was the easy part. But he speaks now

of a *soul*. What, for instance, did the creature see?
Moorland, scrub, veld, or sodden jungle,
desert, wood, the same indigo skies?
The man who fits the eyes has never left

his semi in Cardiff, but he's a master of precision,
nothing's too small, or extinct. Recently
though, a slip in concentration perhaps –
an upright grizzly in the Natural History

has the eyes of a man stranded in his front room,
the telly blizzarding, the fire gone dead;
a bison's head looms out of a wall, dazed,
like a woman just woken, sleep crusting her eyes;

and a pair of monkeys stare out from a London window,
like lovers come to the end, at a loss
in front of what has been, what is to come
(deaf to the whirr and gong of the clock on the hour).

His eyes brim at night from all the detail.
There's a tea-towel over the mirror and it takes him a while
to sleep. *Everything's always awake*, he says.

Allies

I first realised you were not who I'd taken you to be
when I found you sleeping in the middle of a dark afternoon.
Sent home early, ashamed, in tears, I wandered
round the empty house, shambled into your room.
The curtains fell like a shroud around your bed,
around you who never slept, whose job it was to watch over me
but who now lay stirring your own dreams, elsewhere.
Then you opened your eyes, you must've felt my breath,
and looked at me like a patient coming to, resenting
the first face she sees after a deep and bewildering absence.

Then the day your mother died. You lost your tongue
and roamed the house. When you opened doors you saw
us, your children, neither here nor there but somewhere
as tiny figures receding into unlit corners.
We held your life now in our smaller hands
but we could no longer touch you without thinking first.
You spent the nights turning her habits into yours;
putting silk you'd never wear to sleep in drawers,
collecting foreign coins your husband forgot to spend,
perfuming the rooms with leaves that'd take years to die.

And the third time, when we were all sent home early.
I didn't know that room had a door till I saw it shut.
The house had tried to seal itself against us
and even the dog bristled, but my brother, idiot,
never one to listen, listened at the door, then pushed.
I was curious that you came out fully clothed and so quickly,
proud that all you did was zip up your thigh,
flick your hair, look flushed and embarrassingly young.
My sisters stared at the ground, doomed. But me,
I like to think I looked you straight in the eye.

Initiation

Geometry was beyond me. I was a girl and its constancy,
its pure, unbending language felt like punishment enough.
But I liked the soft exactness of a sharpened pencil
and I liked drawing those eternal forms:
rhomboid, trapezium, dodecahedron.
We spent most of that summer upstairs in his room,
him incanting equations, me tracing the shapes
while his mother would bring us muffins and maple
and we'd smell the Stella sweet on her breath.

Evenings began fine, light, with a blackbird
singing in the garden and a man in the kitchen
telling jokes, slapping the table with great flat hands,
flicking open the beer, firing off wild little explosions.
And sometimes we'd hear her humming an old tune.
But as night drew around and corners caved in they would
fall quiet, as if they were being stranded, knew it
but didn't care. Then, only the scratching of my pencil softening
to silence and him beside me murmuring $y = a = pq^2$.

The first time I heard it I rushed to the window to see
if I could see it, the creature, under a wheel or in a trap,
or was it just the cats coming together in their hateful way?
But my eyes wouldn't get used to the dark so I had to stand there,
blindly, hearing it go on and on and on, feeling that
all the things I knew, that once secured this view,
the climbing frame, garden shed, the old swing
had not been strong enough, had simply gone,
vanished into this open mouth, this mother of a night.

When I crept out of his room she was standing in the hallway.
Her feet looked very white, the moon rose high in her toenails,
and her ankles were thin and lonely as wintry stems.
She held her plait like a rope in one hand. We stood
staring at each other and when she opened her mouth
as if to say something I turned and ran, dropping my books
behind me and as I ran I heard them falling, thudding
down the stairs like dead birds, their spines cracking,
the pages loud and broken and useless.

I went back the next day. He opened the front door
and said Hello but it was as if we didn't know each other.
Very slowly I followed him up the stairs, treading the centre
of the steps where the wood was worn and golden. Far away
I could hear her – *O Shenandoah I love your daughter* –
and later, the only light his angle-poise shining
its circle onto our books, open at the same, last page,
and him on the bed, entering me for the first time,
fingering my face, mystified, as if at an impossible equation.

A Hundred Sheep in a Green Field

The way our mother said something
under her breath made us suddenly hush
in the back and not ask why we'd slowed
to barely a crawl or why we were told
to roll up the windows and sit tight
and *Everything is going to be all right.*
Our faces, soon waxy with sweat,
mooned out against the glass as we crept
alongside cars where men, alone
in suits, breathed in and out their own
serene and air-conditioned air.

Slowly, we came upon the scene:
under a big, blue sky
the lovely smell of petrol rose
in seething ribbons,
and a woman in a torn summer dress
was dragging her body across the lanes
where bits of toy, car, family
lay like the remains of a picnic,
and a man's head lay sleeping on the wheel.

Then I saw beyond this
to a hundred sheep in a green field
eating their cheerless way through the earth;
eating, eating, until in time,
I thought, they'll reach the red hot centre
and find themselves falling,
stiff and stupid as tables,
into that burning pit.

The rain started when we crossed the border
and didn't stop once the whole summer.
We had to light fires in every room;
even the sheets smelled of coal.
My sister sat at the window
closing and opening the curtain
onto an empty, shining field.

Dungeness

A man in a black shirt is kneeling in a garden.
He is holding a handful of seed. He looks up.
The sun is humming like a low engine
and all around acres and acres of earth
erupt in sudden tufts of grass
as dry and sparse as sick man's hair.

Sand sieves through the scalp of a doll
whose despised body lies scattered, in bits.
She doesn't know how to die but she's trying.
And the little houses sit like accidents,
their windows broken, their doors open,
guarded by gnomes with hurtful smiles.

Orange iron tracks stop one foot short
of the water's edge. The final carriage
has long since tipped itself down
onto the ocean floor where it's turning
now into a quiet and complicated home
for the fish who pass unflinchingly by.

On the shore the corpse of a baby shark
lies on its back, its cold eye
still seeing, and its penis, open, curls
in surprise on its tender white belly.
In the hollows of dunes sofas
sit and wait like patient guests.

And in that garden three black shirts
hang on a line. The man is planting now.
There's an element of shame in the way
he bows his head as he buries the seeds
deep and deeper under the earth.
He wonders if he'll touch the sleeve, or the collar
or even the lips of his safely dead lover.

The Night We Stole a Full-Length Mirror

I'd have walked straight past if you hadn't said
Look at the moon and held my head in your hands
and turned it slowly round to face a skip,
its broken skyline of one-legged chair, ripped
out floor, half a ladder, till I saw it moving
– so slow, so bright – across the silver glass.
We stood there for ages, a bit drunk,
staring at the moon hanging there
as if it were a kind of street performance
and we an old couple looking on, innocent,
slightly baffled but liking the way it's making
us feel innocent again. A cat jumps out –
and before we know it we're stealing back to my flat,
the great thing like a masterpiece in our hands,
its surface suddenly anxious with knees and knuckles,
the clenched line of your jaw and your lips
kissing your own over and over with curses.
You lean it so it catches the bed and me,
I nudge it with my toe so it won't hold my head.
Switching off the light my skin turns blue
and when you come in on the scene and we see
ourselves like this we start to move like real
professionals (where did we learn to do such things?)
and I watch or rather my head, disowned and free,
watches what our bodies are doing and somewhere
the thought *I can't believe we weren't made for this*
and I can't stop looking even though the ache
in my throat is growing and soon there will be tears
and I can hear you looking and I know what you're
looking at and it doesn't matter but it isn't me.
You left me behind in a bar in Copenhagen St,
the one with the small red lamps and my face, hung
a hundred identical times along the damp-stained
wall, invoking, like some old speaking doll,
the dissatisfaction I come back and back to
and there's this really pretty Chinese waitress
you're trying not to look at while I'm talking to you.
Then you get up and I'm left alone so I lift my head to look
at the man who's been staring at me since I walked in.

He's huge and lonely and lifts his glass and nods
and all the women along the wall break into smiles.
Then you're back and whispering *your breasts your breasts*
and your hands are scrambling up the wet stone
of my back and I imagine the lonely man is there
behind the silver screen sipping his drink,
his eyes thick and moist behind the glass.
I know he's waiting to catch my eye but I won't:
I won't be seen to know I'm being watched.
Not till it's over and we collapse, all of a sudden
and awkward, and the room becomes itself again,
filling the mirror with its things, and our two faces
staring in, calm and dull and self-absorbed.
Then we look at each other and are surprised,
as if we weren't expecting to find the other
here, and the smile is quick, like a nod slipped in
between two conspirators returned to the world
of daylight, birdsong, the good tug of guilt,
before we tilt the mirror up-, sky-, heaven-ward.

HELEN FARISH

Helen Farish writes:

'What we said was less/ than what we saw', writes Eavan Boland in her poem 'The River', implying that there is something beyond language and that language can fail sometimes to haul it in and net it safely on the page. Language is the inescapable layer between 'what we saw' and the articulation of it. But there is of course no clear-cut dividing line: the one runs into the other, which is to say that we both write and are written by language. We construct the poem but the poem also constructs us.

Like most writers, I am at different times frustrated and elated by language. I think of Hélène Cixous accusing language of being both our traitor and our ally. I'm sure every poet can remember poems where the experiences or feelings which occasioned them somehow remained stubbornly out of reach, swimming in watery territory somewhere beyond the poems' boundaries. But if words inevitably and unavoidably mediate those 'poetic feelings about poetic experiences',[1] how can we put them together in such a way that 'what we said' is not less than 'what we saw'? How can we succeed in getting the edges of words to blur, each one to leak out something in excess of what is normally required of it so that the poetic moment brims on the page?

Of the many potential answers to this question one which preoccupies me at the moment is a bareness, a directness of language, choosing 'the real thing' over 'the emblem',[2] employing a disarmingly lucid poetic in the belief that it will do the job of making what is said equal what was seen, that figurative language can be reduced to a minimum. I think to do this in poems and still make them resonate richly with meanings requires no small amount of skill. It also requires a certain amount of courage in the face of the post-modern climate with its prescriptions of irony and parody. I think of Louise Glück's preference for 'simple language' as being best suited to the enterprise of liberating 'by means of a word's setting, through subtleties of timing, of pacing, that word's full and surprising range of meaning'.[3] I cannot claim this by any means for my own work; it remains something to aspire to. I can only admire it when I find it, for example the fourth part of Glück's poem, 'Baskets', where less is so very much more, where the sea is present in the river and the river in the rain.

---

[1] Eavan Boland, *Object Lessons* (London: Vintage, 1996), p. 241
[2] Eavan Boland, *Collected Poems* (Manchester: Carcanet, 1995), p. 120
[3] Louise Glück, *Proofs and Theories* (Manchester: Carcanet, 1999), p. 4

The Contentment of the Lute Maker

Each hour, like a string,
has its own pitch,
and though I compose with wood
I hear the harmony.

Sycamore or beech for the neck,
for the pegs boxwood or ebony,
the ribs curly maple or ash,
pear for the bridge.

I sand, I plane, I reveal
the figure, raise the grain.
I assemble with precision.
With care I carve a rose.

Morning must be flush
with the belly of afternoon;
I choose Swiss pine high-grown
for its dense rings of time.

Contentment is the key
of each slow movement.
My workshop is my stage
and the finished lute never mine.

As afternoon tapers
to the endclasp of evening
the tone is whole,
the day perfectly tuned.

Clytaemnestra and Agamemnon

For my wedding night with Tantalus
what care I spent perfuming my body.
I chose lavender, vanilla, lemon;
loved his slow discovery of each.

Now I chose the white of the almond blossom
Iphigenia would have smelt this spring,
the white of waves my baby would have worn,
the underside of the olive

which blows a ghost colour,
and the whitish brown the fields would be
in the massacre month. Subtle shades
lost on Agamemnon.

The two years I spent weaving I saw only
red, how his body would be
sliced into by the double-edged sword,
the whites wrapping round.

When he returned my hands were whitish brown.
I lay the banquet, smiled. Vulnerable as a baby
he bathed before me, the scum of battle
lathering the silver sides.

His skin was a ghost colour.
Waves splattered on the shore where his ship lay.
Inside me pity curled up tight and blind
as blossom in the bones of a tree.

When he stood the water slipped and sucked.
I heard Iphigenia say *yes, sacrifice him*.
Tantalus said, *remember our new born*.
With a vicious stitch I wove red and white.

His blood's slow discovery of air
drained years of hate. That spring out walking
I could smell it all again. Almond, lemon,
my feet weaving through the groves.

Angela Di Foligno
?1248 – 1309

You have to understand that when I stripped
before the cross, my cross
wasn't in a dark incense-heavy church
but on a hillside of such sweetness,
the blonde grass soft enough to swim in,
and approaching Christ I did indeed
feel as though I was wading,
scents of wild thyme swaying.

I needed to be lighter, to feel
clothes crumpled at my feet.
I had to be naked. It was my penance.
I obeyed. I shook. My body
with all its imperfections next to his.
My wrists, arms, breasts, hips,
my legs, knees, thighs, each part
I accused in turn, concentrating
you don't know how hard.

Then I saw it. The blood. And I drank,
pressing my lips, newly accused,
against his wound. I was there
with Mary Magdalen, his mother and the others,
my mouth drinking and drinking, my lips, Christ,
could have roamed anywhere.

And when the cross entered me I knew
I'd wash the sores of lepers to drink
down the water, knew I'd sleep
on paving stones, rub lice
into home-made wounds, eat ash,
caress nettles into my breasts, break glass
to roll in.
            And the sweetness
was so unbearable I screamed,
the dark church swelling with my ecstasy,
the twitterings of disapproval
transformed in my head to the unimaginable

27

songs of birds invisible in the air but there
like the sin crumpled round my feet, like Christ
inside me saying *There now*
you are full.

Kingfisher

I stood so long by the river
till the long light of day
sank finally into twilight,
till the river's quiet rush
locked me where I stood.
The whirl of thick water
swallowed the swift white
as a snake would a bird;
the slow writhe appalled,
but once confronted
I could not go back.
So I stood long by the river
facing a place
where drownings could occur.
And settling so densely
was the silt of darkness
I could not swear I saw
a bolt of blue flash
along the river's snake-back:
flying as though by colour alone.

Anne Boleyn

I am come hether to accuse no man, nor to speake any thyng
of that, whereof I am accused and condempned to dye, but
I pray God save the king and send him long to reygne over
you, for a gentler nor a more mercifull prince was there never:
and to me he was ever a good, a gentle and soveraygne lorde.

1527

In the afternoon I stripped
to my underwear and lay
fingering each moment.
His visit had been unannounced
but in his wife's chamber I was the one
he danced with. His eyes
followed me like the sun.

And I remember the floor that night
covered in cloth of silk, his black velvet slippers
on the lilies' embroidered gold. I knew
when he unmasked it was my future I'd see.

The gifts started: emerald rings, bows, arrows,
his picture set in bracelets, linen, rich furs,
saddles and harnesses, rubies, diamonds,
pillions in black velvet. He took me to the Tower,
filled my arms with gold plate,
fine black satin.

1532

It was the rain in Calais,
insistent for two weeks,
like his fingers at my bodice,
his jewels at my throat.
The puddles soaked up resolve,
ran it into the brown and swollen sea.

1533

He married me secretly that winter,
unclasped my desire like never before.
His square bed saw me remove
each last thread of gold, thread of silk
till only jewels remained, and the king
created a thousand heirs a night.

Before the coronation fifty barges
took me to the Tower. It was May.
Five months pregnant I chose
rich cloth of gold, and for Westminster
purple velvet trimmed with ermine.
My hair I left loose, but on that day
not even the wind dare disturb me.

I had the peacocks removed before the birth.
I never liked their eerie cries.
Lady Lisle sent me peewits.
My husband planned a tournament and a pageant.
He selected the names Henry and Edward.
I had an altar set up in my room,
read the Bible in French.

When she came he blamed my body
for the daughter, had a mistress
in his square bed by Michaelmas.

1536

I wore yellow when Catherine died,
Elizabeth I dressed in orange satin,
my lying-in chamber I made ochre.
But the Henry inside struck me with pain,
came out as deformed as my future.

On the second day of May they came for me.
Holding our daughter I pleaded with the King.
Had he forgotten the May we first danced,
our summer progresses, Calais,
how he used to watch
if the wind lifted my hem?
But the look in his eyes was as though
humanity wasn't ours to share.

Three hours in the barge to the Tower.
I heard the water and when I closed my eyes
a pavanne.
                    My sweet brother
died because of me. My father and mother
sent no word. Was I not Anne,
little Anne? Had father not kept
the letter in which I promised
I would strive to please him?
Seven years old. Suddenly I remembered
clavichord lessons with Hendrick.

May 19th

6am. A watery breeze.
My window open
as I dress and pray.
My speech is ready.
My hair is dark.
I choose black damask
with an ermine mantle of white.
For my head
a cap of linen.

Whoever Drops Me

That's what I could do, think about my mother's sister.
The tick of a clock, a tea-table to be cleared,
outside a bitter Easter and the slowness of life;
a day steady as spring or regular as clogs
crossing a cobbled yard. That's what I could do:
find quiet passageways back to rooms
where afternoons sat quiet as china dogs
and evening came easy as drifts of late snow.

I could mythologize and flatten
lives as complex as my own to help me cope
this evening, alone, with an adulthood far removed
from the stretched-out stillness of a lake lying like
the purpose of every walk. I want to
hold on to china dogs, to feel safe as
a destination, and whoever drops me
unsmashable.

KATE LING

Kate Ling writes:

'Before Ripening' started as a series of short sketches. They could hardly be called poems. I made no rational decisions about line length, metre, stanza divisions. The only organising principle was that each began with a title which I lifted from a list I found in the back of a book of Baudelaire's prose poems, a list of titles he never got round to using. I was on a train to Paris, six weeks pregnant, eager to start writing some kind of journal of my pregnancy, and with no idea where to start. Setting myself the task of using Baudelaire's titles forced me into areas of imagery I would never have chosen to use, as I spent the next four days in Paris, trying to respond to such titles as 'Fiesta in a Deserted Village', 'Statistics and the Theatre' and 'Mappa Mundi'.

For many months I worked on the poem concentrating mainly on the meaning. By now it was nine sections long, one section for each month of my pregnancy, and I removed Baudelaire's titles, replacing them with numbers. I was starting to crave a shape for the poem which would unite the sections formally, and the first step of this reshaping came when I discovered David Constantine's *Caspar Hauser* and became mesmerised by his three line stanzas. I changed the stanza breaks to fit this model and began to sense the beginnings of a loose but jaunty rhythm, which I liked . . .

> *Before you breathed, my fish, we four went under*
> *The sea, you and me, your father, my beautiful*
> *Mother, filled with the courage of the unborn*
>
> *Wrapped in coats of velvet lined with silk.*

I was near the end of my pregnancy, and the poem had reached a certain point of completion. The poem did not rhyme formally, but there were many haphazard internal rhymes. I liked the tone of the poem. Was it finished? I decided it was, in the same way as I had made many of the decisions during its development – it was intuition, guesswork, but more, I just didn't know what else to do with it. That seemed as good a reason as any to call it finished.

Months after deciding that 'Before Ripening' was finished I began to look at it more critically. There were glaring repetitions, lumpy sections, bits that sounded pretty but made no sense. I wanted to perfect it and I wanted it to have strong formal qualities. It seemed impossible that I could change a word and the more impossible it seemed, the more exciting the prospect of messing about with it became.

First I put the whole poem into iambic pentameter. As I shifted and changed odd words, cut phrases, rearranged lines and stanzas, the poem ceased to exist as an expression of my precious emotions, and became a puzzle. I was now working on the level of words, as a craftsperson. I found developing the rhyme scheme much more difficult as my previous attempts to work with rhyme had been ham-fisted, the rhymes clichéd and often awkward. But the fact that I had lost that emotional link with the poem made the cuts I needed to make in order to accommodate the rhyme scheme much easier to accept. Some ideas just didn't fit any more and if they didn't work formally then they had to go. Often the phrases I decided to cut were weak ideas in the first place. With a rigorous formal approach weaknesses become obvious. The penultimate draft began,

> *Before you breathed, my fish, we crossed the sea*
> *Sleeping in the darkness of the tunnel*
> *Surrounded by the warm wet of the channel*
>
> *My velvet coat wrapped round us like a womb.*

I now had my rhythm and rhyme scheme, but the words on lines two and three were clearly only serving to provide a route to the rhyming word on the end of each line. I doubled back and worked on the beginnings of lines, trying to make them stand up for themselves and not merely as props for the end-rhymes.

Now that I've finished working on the poem I find it hard to believe that I wrote it. I can explain the process by which it developed, but there is still something magical about a final draft, when the poem stands on its own two feet with a structural logic of its own. This is what makes poetry exciting to write, and it's also what makes starting the next poem so daunting.

Before Ripening

I

Before you breathed, my fish, we crossed the sea
lulled by the sound of the train beneath the channel
as we headed south in the darkness of the tunnel,

my velvet coat wrapped round us like a womb.
We slept, and reached the city boundary dreaming
of the shape of Sacré Coeur on the Paris skyline.

In the gallery it felt like we were flying.
The city was encased beneath the floor.
Dizzied by the perspective we ignored

the boulevards, skimmed the perspex sky
and circled the Opera House. Then you and I
stood breathless on the roof, each foot on a cupola

held out our arms and listened to the aria
start gently then come rising through our feet.
Week nine – your pulse a rest before a beat,

the distant sound of a practising musician;
your heart a longitudinal cross-section
of the Palais Garnier's red auditorium;

this second held like the breath of an orchestra
on the cusp of music – on stage the choir
hushed at the start of this, your overture.

II

In the twelfth week we arrange a meeting place.
Those slits that were your gills begin to heal.
This high in the waiting room we watch birds wheel

around the tower, then skim the Walworth Road,
turn at the Elephant, their shape a code,
and the trail of a distant plane defines the air.

Then everything happens quickly – you are there,
caught on the monitor, your fish gills closing,
your hands pulsating with the beat of wings.

III

I'll tell you about some things you don't know yet:
this Black Country, the coalyards closed, the coal
long gone; the Sunday league warming the soil;

your great-grandfather's hard black back, his face
blacked up, the source of your father's amazement;
the sun on steel; the veins of railway lines;

we three bound home along the rigid spine
of motorway; the canal still as mica;
the smell of oranges on our fingers; this light;

a beautiful gas-station half deflated
in December. Mid-January. Winter cold is late.
No frost attacks the plants and still no snow,

no bitter wind comes clawing through our clothes.
Without a coat your father's in his element,
tending these early purple primulas.

I hanker for the frozen ground, sub-zero
temperatures, parameters, but he'd live
in eternal spring, sun on his skin

accepting a single season without question.
Your knees stretch, though I haven't felt a kick.
The sun shines and you turn your back on it.

You like it cinema dark, like midnight railtracks;
like the inside of a tin of black molasses
with the lid on; like the oven; as dark

as a pitshaft, your hand obscured before your face,
like space; so dark it's as dark as that first piece
of coal your great-grandfather picked, with skin

still white; the coal-dark of imagination.
Time's messed up this winter, the body clock
of spring unhinged. On Royal Hill we're shocked

by blossom, and azaleas so soon.
For once I wasn't thinking about you,
forgot about you tucked inside my coat.

I'd dreamt of blood and urine, of meat that floated
beneath a bridge, already going rotten.
In a year this day will be forgotten.

IV

Your heart beats like a pounding horse; a signal,
morse, sent double time; a radar bleep;
like blood inside your ear when you can't sleep;

a whiplash walloping the wind; a thrum
perched on electric lines before a storm;
like putting your hand on a railway line and feeling

a distant train come; like strobes across the ceiling –
the bathroom fan, your head below the surface;
like a tunnel of water filled with surfers;

your heartbeat spools around my tape on an endless
reel to reel. I listen close, with stealth,
a birdegg thief eavesdropping on a pulse.

V

Schönbrunn – the nineteenth week. A chrysalis
hangs from a leaf in the butterfly house.
We breathe humidity and watch small mouths

feed from flowers, their needle-like antennae
dug deep and draining off the thick, sweet honey.
A scarlet butterfly sucks on my neck,

and in the tiergarten storks stand on nests
and stare down at their feet, shocked. I read:
The pelican lives like a gazelle. It feeds

on fish all day. Its golden bruises always show.
While feeding the child will eat the parent's throat.
The seadog sidles the Atlantic in great swathes.

In front of them they mother the great waves.
Young animals cannot swim in the middle
of their birth but see their mothers. They are travelled.

My baby German, born in a new language.
These are the words that I can only guess at,
and you a text that I can't translate yet.

VI

What would I do to save your skin?
Run coatless through the pouring rain,
Stand still before a speeding train,

grip the wing of an airborne plane.
I'd swim a swamp of crocodiles,
photograph top secret files,

cross a desert all the miles
it took to keep you out of danger.
I'd attack a perfect stranger

if you were only slightly injured.
I'd step before a flying bullet,
snatch the rip cord hard and pull it,

take a tiger by the gullet,
kill it, and live to not regret it.
I would die to save your eyes.

VII

Your father knows the secret of photography.
Each day he catches me against new light,
and locked inside his darkroom every night

he develops us on paper like fine skin,
the negative exposed, the print blue-tinged.
Each day's new light is fixed. He can repeat it –

there's nothing we need forget. Week twenty-eight.
My womb is like the surface of the moon,
smooth as an egg, a shifting edge like sand dunes.

The pictures are of space and you the astronaut,
suspended by a thread, turning somersaults.
Orient yourself. See this wedge of sun

pass across your growing field of vision.
We hang your picture by the luminous globe
your father bought. Light tears through tiny holes

in the blue sea and splits Colombia,
the Gulf of Guinea, Indonesia,
the Pacific – your head a map of this great ocean,

your veins like thin red lines of wind direction,
eddying. Here comes the storm again:
outside, the blood red tree, beyond, the rain.

VIII

Four days and nights it rained, the water rising
beyond the banks, my mother and father stuck
as the Vale of Evesham filled up like a bucket.

Week thirty-one. I'm all at sea, feet wet   —
like the woman on the news who saw her carpets
rise and drift towards the door. She trawled

for shoes, small boats as they sailed along the hall,
then sat all night upstairs in darkness, waiting
for her furniture to find its feet again.

Fish, soon you will begin your final journey,
will surface soon, will be amphibian briefly.
What are you like? To me you are long limbs,

the single tree I studied from the window,
as verbs were conjugated all around me,
as glaciers were explained, as Mrs Ramsay

looked up from her knitting and gazed across the sea.
You're an apple growing on that single tree,
an apple in the soft skin of an arm,

the smell of apple flesh kept in the warm
corner of my desk, a pip in my teeth.
Describe this apple. See how impossible it is.

IX

Week thirty-eight. Time burst in like a sofa
through a door, the crockery boxed, the plants uprooted,
the flat packed up, just us and an empty room.

We'd grown. Yours was the last layer of skin
to fit. Meanwhile your elbow's quite distinct,
your birth inevitable as the workmen's wagon.

Their sleeves rolled, double parked, ramp down,
they shift us with the skill of seasoned midwives.
Your father's in the garden burning leaves,

flames lifting their black dust into the sun,
and me, I am the girl with the loudest voice,
singing her song along the Rue de Rivoli.

Thirteen

I stood at the stern of the Larne-Stranraer ferry watching the wake
    grow wider, as Ireland sank
like an abandoned vessel. We were sick, like divers who surface too
    fast, each of us crossing the liquid border
in his own chamber, and in the morning the car smelled of oil and
    fish, the heat of yesterday's paper.
I played *I Spy* through the docks but stopped as we passed the beach
    to watch a stranded dog
bark across the sea as he found his rock surrounded. The mainland.
    In my new school I could no longer
pronounce my name, and answering my number in the register, sent
    thirteen rippling round the room.

Back home things were changing. A boy I knew was dead, found
    holding the gun. That summer
we both turned thirteen, his hands had grown so big they'd beaten
    the rest of him to manhood.
We'd been left alone in the caravan. When I asked him what he
    wanted to be he didn't answer,
but picked at the crack in the formica table with the nail of his trigger
    finger. As rain spilled out
of our disused buckets, he dealt the cards, tossing out hearts, flicking
    over the thirteen spades, guessing
what was coming next. We both stared out of a different window,
    waiting for someone to walk in.

The night we heard the news the stove and fridge were in the hall.
    The kitchen floor of the new house
had subsided into clay. My brother sat in the hollow room drawing
    the boy's face from memory.
We knew we wouldn't be going back. After the shock, silence closed
    around us like the sea.
I patched up my accent, kept my mouth shut.

Trigonometry

There were things I didn't understand at school like equations, and
    how I knew the boy's religion
without being told, and the power of n and what men did in the
    Antrim Hills on dark nights, not by torchlight
but in the gathered shadows of their thick coats, warmed by ardour.
    I did not know what that meant,
but linked it to a church we passed on the way to Belfast.

There were things I didn't understand like *sin* and *cosin*, and how I
    knew the politics of the boy before
I knew his name, and tangents, and why the burnt-out bus that
    blocked the road was still there long after
the upholstery had stopped smouldering and why we were diverted
    from the route we always drove
and had to take the back road home from Belfast.

I didn't understand angles, and why I thought the necklace the boy
    gave me was dangerous and how
the value of x and y could be deduced by those who'd learnt the
    formula for homework and why
my father's stolen car was found, tyres bald, the boot bust open,
    abandoned in a quiet street in Belfast

and why couldn't the boy and I stop laughing as we tried to measure
    angles round a point, our desk cut
by a square of sun and why, when suddenly our elbows touched, did
    we keep our eyes fixed on the teacher,
then head at the bell across the triangle of playground, the boy on the
    hypotenuse, me on the opposite side?

ROGER MOULSON

Roger Moulson writes:

I started writing because I kept re-reading poetry. When I read the Elizabethan poets it was as if they were in the same room. This is talking to the dead, I told myself. Not only would I share some longing or anger of theirs and say Yes! as their words struck me – they asked me questions. What do you think? What do you feel? Later on I was drawn to the work of Hugh MacDiarmid and found myself arguing with him until I read everything he wrote.

Sometimes I find poetry daunting to read. I avoided Milton for various reasons, then one day I picked up *Paradise Lost* and skated as fast as I could over its slightly repellent latinate surface till I suddenly felt, Oh! I've just gone over a crack in the ice. *The mind is its own place* . . . I stopped and read the passage more slowly . . . *receive thy new possessor – one who brings/ a mind not to be changed by place or time./ The mind is its own place, and in itself/ can make a Heaven of Hell, a Hell of Heaven.* How pride aspires to power, how power is abused. He enters his character's mind in the same way as Satan is *constrained/ into a beast*. The passions of the English Civil War are in it and his own self knowledge. Exact descriptions such as how Satan was briefly *stupidly good* watching Eve. The sentences are long and ambitious, but the bold enjambement and metre carry me forward. I found it liberating. I still find long chunks of the poem rather overblown, but it is a poem I now respect and go back to.

I read contemporary poetry the same way. I read quickly and see if anything makes me stop or want to go back over it. Compare Milton's hard surface with the unattractive irony and cleverness of much written recently. Both have boring bits, this despite the fact a lot of current writing is in lyric form, an attempt to avoid what is felt to be a loss of intensity in longer poems. Sometimes I notice passages that hold me have very simple words, single syllables maybe, as in the first Milton quote above. Sometimes the poet comes up with something I didn't expect. A last line that makes me turn round, look back and wonder how I got there. Or funny seriousness like MacNeice's . . . *bus after tall bus comes/ with an osculation of yellow light, with a glory like chrysanthemums*, indeed the whole poem with its unpromising title, 'An Eclogue for Christmas'. The cumulative power of Emily Dickinson's voice, so arresting that after reading a few poems I look up half expecting her to materialise in front of me. Or I discover one poem I like by a poet I can't otherwise get on with – Browning's wonderful 'Child Roland to the Dark Tower Came'. I was taken aback when I came to read Henrysoun's 'Testament of Cresseid' to find he explains how he came to write the poem and makes that explanation part of the poem. *I mend the fire and beikit me about,/ then tuik ane drink my spreitis to comfort,/ and armit me well frae the cauld thereout:/ to cut the winter nicht and mak it short,/ I tuik ane Quair* (book), *and left all uther sport,/ writtin by worthie Chaucer glorious,/ of fair Cresseid, and worthie Troylus.* I don't know the secret of poems that stop me dead. I *think* it has to do with the poet listening to what the poem is trying to become, listening to thoughts instead of trying to speak them.

Listening is part of reading. I voice words to hear them in my head. I talk to myself. I listen to what people say in cafés, on the phone, the snatches of song they sing, late night sounds of drunks, cars, wind and water, the sounds that make up a silence. Reading is an ongoing conversation I need to have to write.

Waiting for the Night-Rowers

Word is the rowers start and square their blades.
The hills attend. They're crazy for release,
for night to find its marker pen and cross
them out with clear firm strokes in parallel
so they can cool and breathe and be forgotten.

The view's an array of pockets lined with pinks
and saturated greens filling with shadows
of velveteen. A mist is rumour of their breath,
rehearsal of stroke, cheating the ears of those
that dread the silent dipping of the blades.

Windows reflect the skyline and pass the torch
to factories moulding matter into things,
lulled with repeated motions, easy desires
for sex and cigarettes, flick, flicker, gone
in drawing in and slow express of air.

A steel flue tapers like some endless waist
cooling what passes in and out, solids
turning into smoke that's dark by day and pale
by night. Now to be breathed, down the long strain
of ribs, is wanting's blue turned indigo.

Lungs work to reach the end of all their lines
till every throat goes dry and soughs like wind,
for nothing runs the length of violet
and if it did no voice would stretch that far
except the rowers' song, too low to hear.

Now moons illuminate the inlets and fumes
stream brownly over stone as evening pushes
bodies into doorways. Light gentles around
largenesses, leaves some of itself behind
against the stare of faces bending to the water.

Pulling its slugs of oxygen cold wind
feeds fire through the channels, flame without light.
Lovers use lamps to measure emptiness.
Hungry for cold fetchings, fixings, gettings,
they brave the approaching silence of the blades.

They seek the usual intensest colours
and ask, Will it be soon? and practise standing
very still to imagine the force and calm of love.
They empty themselves entirely, prepared
to be displaced, to bear the passage of the rowers.

A Good Time for Sea-Life

Framed by pictures of whales, sharks,
the varieties of jellyfish, she sits in her hut.
What's the best time for sea-life? I ask.
After a spell of fine weather, she says,
and we might get a plankton bloom,
and it has to be calm and a high cloud,
no shine so nothing reflects but your face.
If you want something different,
if you don't know what you're after,
night is a good time. The boat leaves at ten.

Me and the others, clothes heavy with sand,
give her our tickets and we pitch
through a tunnel of powerful light, past seals
and past jellyfish she nets up to show us.
Then we stop, For the dolphins, she says,
and by the way my name's Kate and this
is a good night, smooth water, and dolphins
are here. And they are. Or they're rocks.
When she peels off and dives she makes
no reflection. She calls, Why don't you join me?

I do. It's so cold in the sea's gleaming black
there's no time to think between yelling
as if I see a glass dropped, a table walked into.
What I see is a creature, a woman, a fish,
markings of phosphor, a swerving of thoughts,
a ribby thing saying, Ooh, isn't it lovely.
Next day I long for the sound of her pleasure,
the water she swims through. I say, Kate!
She says, If you know what you're after
night is a good time. The boat leaves at ten.

The Wooden Piano

Its makers wanted most to learn to hear, and chose
to learn by building it, shaping each piece by hand.
Two things were difficult, but no one said,
hiding anxieties under leaf and branch.
For hammers, jarrah wood. Tock tock, gung gung.
They only spoke at evening as the piercing blue
flooded the mallee and black peppermint.
For string, they said, the stringybark in our backyard
will do. They twined it, waxed it, pulled it tight.
Straight after morning it was always evening.

Ironbark rang, and still the blue was creeping in
through dusty leaves for they had not invented felt.
They said, We'll make the keys from scribbly gum.
If it were evening all our lives, said one with ears,
we'd never finish. A candelabra
was too complicated, they all agreed, and
unnecessary. The rest was easy, pedals
smooth to touch. When it was finished, they waited
for the longest evening of the year to flow
through tuarts, woollybutts and flooded gums.

The one with ears played klung klung tlock tlock,
a melody her fingers found. Oh, play some more,
they cried, and turn your ears to find that sweetness
in the wood we worked. She played. She swayed. They lay
and listened as she pedalled and felt sounds
plucking at their bones. If we had evenings every day
as long as this, they said, we'd learn to hear so well
we'd spend our lives in listening and say, This
is our work. How it must hurt to really hear.
Klung klung, she played, plink plink, kaloom kaloom.

The Glass of Water

Amazed to find the thing it most desires
light strikes.
Glass rings around it.
The contents accept their shape
but do not own it
as if shape's the need to be held.
Water does not concern itself
which one holds
and which is held.
The glass stands on the ghost of itself.
It shines a beam through shadow
speaks of volume
of a single column.
Water waits to run.
It breathes into the mouth of air.
When it's most still
it is compelled towards the other always.

A Field of Stones

The rain has cleaned us
and soon a frost will pencil in our edges.
Our labouring in the dark to heave ourselves
from bedrock, to get thrown up.
It seems so long ago.
We call ourselves the land's surf.
Who if they really see us does not love us a little?

Not all have eyes, a flat stone says.
I heard a tractor driver say
You sit there like birds along the furrows.
What are you waiting for?

Who ever heard of a stone aching?
Any that say so cannot be true stones.
Some believe in a final landfall, a land of basalt.
We believe in becoming more like ourselves.

We don't want to fly like birds,
says the flat stone, All that flapping.

We want to fly without any weight.
It only needs one of us to do it.
Just think, if all the stones suddenly lifted up,
people would say, The land is sinking.
The land is leaving the stones in a field of air.

The flat one says, They'd say the stones
want to fly into our mouths and kill us.
The stones want to wear coats of blood.

Or it might be night
so our flight darkens the stars.
We'd make patterns no one else would see.
Next morning they would look at the field
and say, That field used to be covered with stones.
The farmer has cleared them
and the earth looks better.

Field Guide to the Birds of Britain and Europe

Plate 1: The male great northern diver's
always first and swims in summer plumage
beside its double, dressed for winter
both on the same wave, motionless.
Loud screams and yodels, says the text,
On breeding waters, maniacal laughter.

The albatross is steering clear
of mariners and such. The crow's
not doing anything disgusting.
While doves are listening for the obvious
rhyme, the grounded lark keeps stumm,
and swans are all reduced to scale.

There's a king but no queenfisher,
a night but not a dayingale,
many sparrows, one sparrowhawk,
three different bustards, one sole shag
and a display of tits, mostly male,
blue, bearded, marsh, coal, crested, great.

They all share the same piece of sky.
The red and black kites, the hen, marsh
and Montagu's harriers, the booted
eagle, the honey and common
buzzards fly up the page in perfect
formation, each with its markings.

Five hundred birds in full colour.
They fly auspiciously from right
to left. Or sit in puddles stuck
to their reflections. Or perch on twigs
detached from trees. Or, standing rapt,
their feet grip the white of paperspace.

KATHERINE FROST

Katherine Frost writes:

In the writing of these poems, most of all with the snake sequence, I was thinking among other things about the way in which poetry can explore ideas. I had been interested in the uses of narrative, which can simultaneously stand in its own right and serve this other end. I had also been mulling over a remark of Elizabeth Bishop's, addressed to certain 17th-century writers but of significance for her own development: their purpose she said was to portray 'not a thought, but a mind thinking'. More recently I had been drawn to the poems of C. K. Williams in which he pushes a similar notion to extraordinary limits, pursuing the twists and convolutions of the process to a point where it becomes also a meditation on what is observed, which is rendered immensely more complex and mysterious than it first seemed.

In parallel to this were reflections on the range of resources syntax can offer for tracing nuances of thought and feeling.

'Fortunate Episodes' arose in part from incidents which I did actually witness. But it arose as much from an *Encyclopaedia Britannica* entry and from folklore, travelbooks, museums. I wanted first quite simply to be able to tell the stories: I was fascinated by the fascination of snakes, the hold they have over us. But as the sequence took shape, it moved from a more direct focus on 'what happened' in the opening poem, towards a more thoroughgoing psychological narrative. I was then finding that while the earlier phase lent itself to relatively shorter sentences and simpler construction, the latter drew on syntax that was both more elaborate and more disrupted.

The germ of the final poem came to me as a single winding sentence: it pleased me that this one sentence could follow my snakekeeper from her outside, public world, into her hidden private world, and then beyond that to what was to me at that point wholly unexpected, the secret life of the snakes. The bones of that sentence are still there as the third of the four 'sentences' that make up the poem. As this crystallised, themes were emerging that have to do with our relationship to mystery and otherness, the solitary 'something' about the snakes (and the snakekeeper) which has us, on the one hand, insatiably, graspingly curious, and on the other wanting to have it bite back, to resist being wholly known. The extended syntax, serial relative clauses with dysjunctions and interpolations, seemed to offer a means to take in both the psychological movement and the range of material I was after.

Fortunate Episodes

after the unfortunate episode in the Garden of Eden, most
thought of snakes is of envenoming . . .

The Snakekeeper

Already we adore her.
                We wait in hot rows, our legs
                            dangling down. As she

strides about her little pit, her stick
                with its pointy
                            birdbeak jabbing

at earth and stones, finding snakes
                where there were none, our fear's
                            delicious. And when

the long beak goes out
                to loop up a yard or so of oiled flex
                        and lay it at her heel

our calves tingle for her
                as if she were treading the high wire.
                      We know it will strike.

But the mamba doesn't strike. With a
                lack of fuss a glacier might envy,
                    the nailhead

pushes away, the unswerving whiplean
                muscle, its body, shrugged after,
                    as if there

were a tunnel there, a darkness
                it can see and we can't. It's almost
                    at the limit

of her reach when the metal beak
                sneaks out again, snaps up
                                the lank thing and drops it

back at her heel. She wants us
                to understand, a snake's not careless
                                with its powers. Also

what she can do, her chin says that.
                The snake betrays nothing of itself,
                                it pours away

out of her story as before
                into that tunnel of its imagining.
                                Again she picks it up

and again it pours away. Most of us
                when we truly want something,
                                can't quite live it

all through, a child even, long after
                the rest of him has given itself
                                to sleep, will have a

cheek muscle that twitches
                remembering milk: the mamba's body
                                wants one thing. We can't

not look, trapped – in terror
                for her, in the snake's need
                                not to be there.

And she won't stop.
                She'll have her way no matter what.
                                Suddenly we're sick –

with her, ourselves, the whole
                sorry show. A prayer –
                                it does seem

a kind of prayer – shivers between us
        in noon heat.
                Finds an answer –

a move so quick, we almost doubt
        we have seen it –
                the mamba rears,

homes on her knee. A sigh
        like consent
                slips from the benches.

Of course. We knew. Her khaki's
        lined. We don't see
                the snake go.

Molesnake

What is it she's bringing, what
　　　　more can she be wanting from us,
　　　　　　stepping forward

with palms spread wide – so
　　　　biblical her gestures I think,
　　　　　　push the thought

away, of Mary holding out
　　　　the broken Christ – for her arms
　　　　　　have a burden

compliant as pulled toffee,
　　　　silk-sullen as a girl's plait,
　　　　　　trailed

over them? It's the colour
　　　　of sunlight on a gun. She says
　　　　　　'Who wants to stroke it?'

A molesnake has cunning bred for the quick
　　　　underlife of stones,
　　　　　　no need

for venom. Even so there's a
　　　　pause – before three
　　　　　　rows of children

surge to the pit wall, a girl's
　　　　taut 'Who's afraid?'
　　　　　　Our snakekeeper's

a priestess at the altar rail, pointing
　　　　a way for the smallest,
　　　　　　offering

to each in turn, with a kind of
　　　　stern complicity, a place
　　　　　　on the slack

loops to lay one doubting
            finger, the heel of a palm.
                        I'm afraid

for the snake. But for now
            this is all they want,
                        they don't yet want

to hurt it, just to touch. And when they
            have touched they wander
                        in ones and twos

back to their seats, and some are
            silent and some not quite
                        silent, but all

the boastfulness has gone, they hold
            the snakefeel
                        inside them, as if

something had been satisfied.
            One, turned aside from the rest,
                        staring

at his hand – held out stiff before him.
            What print might he
                        find there?

Serpentes, of the Order Squamata . . .

In the dim hall where they're housed
           she sets before us her tribe Serpentes:
                which began

as lizard, but got down
           into the rind of the planet,
                where the gaps are, let go

arms, legs, voice, eyelids, a lung –
           learned to live
                with what's on offer.

She numbers its poisons:
           the kind that makes you
                bleed from every hole –

you die bruised black all over;
           the kind that scrambles what the nerves
                tell each other,

the powerlines cancel like a war –
           you're crushed out of
                breath by your ribs;

the kind that goes straight to your heart
           and stops it.

                And when
the last of us has filed out,
           her creatures are safe under glass,
                when she's checked

the heat and the oily drinking pools
           and let in the silly, scrambling mice
                whose shrieks

the snakes can't hear – when she's home,
           she'll tell her man
                about the coupling;

about how – it may be just after
                    the hibernation sleep that
                                        could have become its last,

or it may be just before each by itself slips down
                    to a dark it can't choose
                                        to wake from –

the male finds the female
                    by the taste of the earth where she's been,
                                        which he sips

with his liquorice twist of
                    tongue, spooling in and up
                                        to the alert

hidden place on his palate
                    that came into being to know this,
                                        the slick of pheromones;

about how, when he has found her,
                    he laps his body along her body,
                                        head

to fluent tip and moulds it to hers;
                    and maybe he takes her neck
                                        in his mouth

as the cobra does – and rears kelim feints
                    to sway with her own; or maybe
                                        he steadies her

with abortive hind limbs, a rump of pelvic girdle,
                    as the python does;
                                        either way –

her throat, her underbelly bared, reaching
                    for his unarmed caress –
                                        he clasps her also

from the inside with a
                hemipenis – its spinules,
                                flounces, calyces.

There can be, our snakekeeper
                will remind her man, neither shy
                                nor ecstatic

closing of eyes –
                only a glance, as past a mirror,
                                and an echo through each

lidless, voiceless escaped lizard:
                something not yet
                                pared from the genome,

that's made it this far,
                easing from cool cells
                                a windfall grace.

SCOTT VERNER

Scott Verner talks to the editors:

'Let's start with what poetry is not. I used to be a journalist, and poetry is not journalism. Journalism makes no requirement from the reader or listener. Everything is there, splat on the page. Fiction moves one step closer to poetry because it invites the reader to participate in the making of the story. But poetry requires the reader, doesn't invite, it *requires* the reader to collaborate in making the poem.

'Reading Pablo Neruda is like reading James Joyce in technicolour. Pablo is a voice of nature, so close to the sea and wheat and wine and to elementals. What is also important about him is his wildness, his lack of inhibition, tempered by humility. He can let anything out, which I envy very much, and yet he walks that invisible tightrope between being wild and being on the other hand disastrously self-indulgent. 'Heights of Macchu Picchu' is extraordinary – bigger than 'The Waste Land' – I think it's the major achievement of the twentieth century. Eliot was walking in back alleys. Pablo was, as he says, plunging his 'turbulent and gentle hand into the genital quick of the earth'.

'Medardo Rosso grabbed me by the throat in a friendly way, the way Pablo did. At his Whitechapel exhibition I was totally arrested, stopped as if my feet had been nailed to the floor. I know that a lot of his early sculptures are sort of old fashioned, three-dimensional representations, but the character in their faces expresses Rosso's powerful compassion which is also angry but never sentimental. And when I saw his later work, it was as if the sculptor had walked away five minutes before and might soon come back and do some more. It looked like something that was making itself right then and there. There was the head of a prostitute called 'The Flesh of Others' done in wax and it was grotesque, yet it had the recognisable features of a terrible woman, or a pitiful woman. There was also the head of a sick child – 'Il Bambino Malato' – and the child's head was melting, you could almost see the brains coming through, the damaged brains. And somehow these sculptures reminded me of my own childhood.

'I used to run away from home regularly, just to get the hell away, and I would go to Big Cypress in the Florida swamps and live by myself until I felt ready to go back. I knew how to live in the wild. I carried a magnifying glass so I could make fire, and an army blanket to keep the mosquitos away. I would roll myself up in it like a mummy at night. And I rejoiced living in this wildness. I was being the me I wasn't allowed to be anyplace else. That's another good thing about poetry, when I write poetry I'm me.'

The Sound of My Head

After 'Il Bambino Malato', a child's
head in beeswax by Medardo Rosso

On my birthday I come in from hiding
in the cold sand under the house
where I've been talking to my friends, the lizards.
Pale sand caked on switch-welts is my new set of ribs.
She says now I'm four, stop crying.

I taste somebody's piss like pennies
on my lemon-coloured birthday cake
and I pretend not to know I'm their animal.
They weigh each feather in my head again,
set some alight, some adrift.

I want to cry with a fish hawk's voice
that's the same sound as the sky tearing.
If I'm quiet as a cricket in a brush fire
they'll laugh at their little birthday joke.
Or she'll break my face for talking crazy.

Maybe I was born crazy, gone fizzy in the head
like a melon left too long in the sun.
That's what they say, doing those things that hurt.
I think of the little toenails on my dried rabbit's-foot
and decide to bury it in the morning.

When I retch on my mother's deep-throat kiss
she says the brown bitter stuff in my ears
is the turds of scorpions that nest in my head while I sleep.
They sting my brain to make mad dreams
and if I wake them at night I'll die.

She yells I'm more stupid every day,
asks can I feel my brain shrinking?
Sometimes I stand off to one side,
shake my head, scared to hear a rattle.

Her Large Smile

*After 'La Grande Rieuse', the plaster
head of a woman by Medardo Rosso*

Coming so soon after the stomach pump
my sister's radiance
is like a sequinned sheet in a morgue.

Like the sun caught in a rain puddle
her smile's too big for her face.
Her eyes, still trying to find their way home,
bond with mine in a flash of acetylene.

Bothered by a breeze or distant voices,
she shatters like a thermometer.
Out of sharp splinters her rage
runs off in all directions.

I can't build a rapport with lightning
but I want to help her, remind her
I'm as close to her shivers as she is –
tremors from childhood quakes:
when someone said 'smile' she flinched,
'sit in my lap' and she wailed.

She announces plans for a famous career –
gathering spider webs deep in the pine woods
which she'll carry home intact
in her miraculous hands,
then melt them gently
to replenish the tears of lost children.

Unaware of the weight of her silent mouth
she hits me head-on with a large smile
that bruises the back of my eyes.
I'm scared what might happen after sundown.

A Lick of Mortality

For Lani

Fresh venom of a diamondback rattlesnake
tastes like wild
orange juice squeezed
from the fruit of a feral
tree. Acidic, more sour than sweet
and alive
the pus-coloured juice congeals.

Fizzy with jism and spunk, I'm a teenage snake
hunter weekends (venomous and benign)
for zoos, laboratories. My vipers
die in captivity, their poison
pharmaceuticalized to save those snakebitten.
Little money, but I like to breathe
wildness, often feel immortal.

In wire grass flatwoods a strong hike
southeast of the Oklawaha where
Otter Creek ponds out, the young sun's
a blood blister on the water. A leopard
frog shrieks in a red-bellied mud snake's
mouth just outside the maidencane
and then I see the rattler. Ten steps away.

A granddaddy, his broad wedge head
points at me. Coiled to strike, he rattles,
a clickety drybone buzz that convulses.
Four light lines on his face, his back
black diamonds in cream on a ripe olive
field. Eye contact: pupils vertically elliptical.
I wish I were so handsome, not so scared.

I've surprised him at home
asleep on the dome of a gopher hole.
He feints a strike or misses, I check
his neck with my snake hook stick,
pick him up behind his head
and he's heavy, longer than I am tall.
When I reach for my burlap bag to put him in

he coils around my shoulder,
neck, slaps my face with his rattle
and shits himself, nothing personal.
Holding his head to drop him in my sack,
but clumsy, I squirt his fang glands on my arm.
He must've gone hungry for a week or more
to carry so much poison in his head.

I lick his venom off my wrist,
its thickness sticks on my unforked tongue
and now I won't send him to the lab. Besides,
I've got no jingle in my pocket
for the Greyhound, so I turn him loose.
When you hitchhike home eighty miles
a rattler in a sack can be an indiscreet companion.

Blue Grass

After 'Calvin Klein's Obsession'
by Ciaran Carson

Very personal, of course, as blue grass is for me the texture of fur-
lined kisses we wash down with Southern Comfort and 7-Up, passing
wild honkytonk mouth-to-mouth, lying flat out, butt naked

in the back of my old Chevrolet pick-up truck parked deep down
in the blossom of the pecan grove where you want to lick the sticky
        air
and I'm deep in my sweetheart Daisy Mae, riding every wiggle

in the banjo's bass line, while she does her thing with the fiddle's
swing and the guitar's yee-haw! choruses, as the boys in the band
rev it up real good – you can feel a hard sweat coming on –

the squeeze box trembles, pulses and pants, shudders and climbs again
as she and I roll over together so the other can see the stars
bounce against the shaking tambourine's slap, tap, and jingle

while the drummer caresses skins with soft sliding brushes, and
        somebody
blows a hillbilly kazoo, a duet with acoustic guitar, and now
all the players pull in real tight, everybody wants to finish together

when live on the radio clear as a bell from Nashville Tennessee
you can hear the bass player groan out loud when his deep E string
        goes twang!
the same time Daisy Mae says the rubber has.

The Study of Air

I can't rightly say
    when I commenced the study of air
        but likely on the far side
of learning to tie my shoes
    as one skill seems
        the left hand of the other
when the tangle
    of an intangible loosens
        by seeing the invisible in motion.

Maybe it starts with snakes
    of air
        writhing off a hot tin roof
or a plume of turbulence from a candle.
    I take no interest
        in circumstantial evidence
like dust, rain or
    tree bend. Just
        air, itself, in action.

A fox won't see a chick
    stock-still on the heath,
        and a cloud chamber
perceives particles only in motion.
    So I can't see
        air
that's not moving or going too fast
    for my eyes.
        Outdoors is usually impossible.

The trick is to look at
    nothing
        but the space in front of my eyes
and pull back from
    any object of sight
        to focus precisely
on a section of
    mid-air
        within reach or across the room.

I see air shrivel, cascade
        on a cold window,
                an ankle-deep creek of cool air
tumble down the stairwell,
        a stepped waterfall. My
                easy breath billows uncoloured smoke
but blown rings
        vanish
                like motes in a blink.

I like to watch pin-feathers
        fall to the floor –
                they daub a trail
like a squirrel's tail in snow.
        Above the soft crown
                of a new-born infant
floats a chain
        of pulses,
                lotus-shaped.

It takes some practice
        to see vibrations of sound in air.
                A bass drum looks
like a pineapple. A violin,
        badly-bowed, a ravelled sleeve.
                Now that I can recognize
your voice on sight, would you
        pleasure my eyes with the shapes
                of the vowels in 'bougainvillaea'?

Frogsong

for Greta Jensen

I'm just a kid
from way down south of Apalachicola
where itty-bitty treefrogs sing all night long
and all the feathered take it up before dawn.

The only needle-noise is a doppler drone
from that minuscule vampire named anopheles.
Endowed with neither webs nor down,
I sling my hammock in a cypress crown

well aloft of skeeters and no-see-ums
in the manner of the Mikasukis,
the tribe of Big Cypress swamps and pine barrens,
a scent of waterlilies and woodsmoke

on their fawn-eyed flirty daughters.
With Draco above, gators below
and suspended sixty feet in between,
I attend the arias of amorous amphibia:

so many ways to say I want you.
A chorus of Peepers is a jingle of sleighbells,
the Bird-Voiced whistles for Fido,
and Squirrel Frogs imitate mallards.

The Cricket Frog's love song is a thumbnail
strumming scales on the teeth of a comb.
The Green Treefrog, a coloraturo,
turns yellow belting bel canto

and the Barking Frog doesn't bow-wow
but burps, a canine cough
like a dog with a frog in his throat.
There's a dandified denizen of the barrens,

lavender stripes on pool-table green,
who doesn't bother to sing, only grunts.
His mother thinks he's just like his father.
That little tan guy on the scarlet bromeliad

encodes his croon in dots and dashes
like a playful breeze on telegraph keys.
The Little Grass Frog, who fits on two-bits
with plenty of change left over,

pings like a porter's bell in a third rate hotel
so high you're surprised you can hear it.
The Barking and the Green sometimes interbreed,
their offspring resembling both lovers,

the shape of one in the skin of the other
in a climate that dissolves biology.
And when a susurrus of wind
in loblolly pines fetches fragrance

from a magnolia in oestrus
my own voice goes sprung,
turns slippy, skids
from treble to baritone.

PETER DANIELS LUCZINSKI

Peter Daniels Luczinski writes:

I wrote poetry at school with some sense of purpose and some discouragement. I read current poetry and read about it, but the poetry world in the seventies seemed nothing but pointless controversy, with apparently no way to learn the craft. Besides, if I was to write poetry honestly I knew I had to deal with being gay. Studying English for a degree (and covering myself with gay liberation badges) did nothing to suggest poetry was still writeable. Gradually, I found poems wanted to be written, but I was nearly thirty when I met someone committed to poetry reading and writing, who crucially encouraged me.

Most of the poems here arrived more or less whole, starting with some shape and an idea of what they were about. Sometimes a poem builds up in small pieces like a jigsaw, which can take years, but it usually needs a stanza shape or other structural principle early on, even if that gets changed. 'Breakfast', 'Policeman' and 'Mall of Mammoths' already existed in time and space as events, and finding the form practically created the poem. Others arose out of insomnia, with help from a biscuit tin of magnetic poetry words.

Whole poems made of them come out like crossword clues, but I pick five words and start writing something that includes them all. I've mixed several vocabularies (Shakespearean Insults, Astrology, Shopping List, Office, and just Magnetic Poetry). This can be a challenge (wanton, Saturn, spaghetti, photocopy, sunset), and results in many unreadable exercises, but it's a way into that 5 a.m. unconscious mind. Good poems must come from wherever good poems come from anyway, and I keep a couple of recent notebooks in the tin, to anchor random words with actual observations.

I try to revise ruthlessly, questioning everything including the form, and sacrificing good words, rhymes, images, for the sake of better ones. But this is hard to do alone. I need workshops, to road-test the poem in the traffic of other people's readings. Reading aloud is essential anyway, for the feel of it in the mouth; but at one workshop I've attended, each poem would be sight-read by someone else, which indicated stumbling points or failures to come across, and even a terrible reading showed how well the poem survived. Workshopping depends on trust, and you even have to take notice of people's hobby horses. I get annoyed when I'm told you can't use the word 'soul' in a poem, but it's more use to consider how necessary it is; and if it's essential, how to make it so good that someone like that might be convinced. Confidence in the work is half the job, the other half is doing it well enough to justify that confidence.

Up

To welcome in the springtime, the curve of the earth
has turned itself our way round – it encourages
our sense of up, the upright rightness of the sun,
because we almost know where we're going now.

It's catching the right bus by guesswork, finding
the yellow blob daisies come up again, in spite
of the incomplete sun that doesn't make a climate
and the devil's hoofprints marching on the land.

Down is not the other side, the never-never hemisphere
with seasons of its own: a globe can go any way
up. The true down is down to the ground: the coin
that comes up sunnyside, slips down the drain.

Here we are, a few thin miles from space:
we want to get up to the sun and the summer, it's
where we're flying, heavier than air. It's up
to us what we get up to – so get up, get it up, go.

Policeman, Stoke Newington

Standing close up to a policeman,
I can get a free look at his
uniform, its unrevealing midnight matt cloth
and silvery buttons, its clever gussets,
and places for his walkie-talkie,
yes, his walkie-talkie tucked under his tunic.
Serious tailoring.

He glances at me sideways,
the expressionless professional
caught in this personal necessity
here at the cash dispenser in the street,
as if performing a secret habit: *Don't be ashamed,*
I could tell him, *It's a normal function, we all do it.*

Satisfied, taking a single circumspect motion
to finish his transaction and reinsert
his wallet in its place, he walks on,
a bobby in a helmet, upright in a naughty world:
he's a policeman with money, stowed
in the safest pocket in the street.

Liverpool St

Meeting at unappointed times, crossing the marble floors
of the refurbished terminus, we celebrate with food, choosing
station pastries or cartons of burger-fries; and we talk
on the train, or sometimes we don't; sometimes that matters,
for reasons of living together, making our way home.

Tonight on the five-forty-five, the couple sitting opposite
get working on separate crosswords like in-trays of invoices,
till one anagram calls out for the full attention of two;
and silently they distribute all of the concatenations,
finding between them the unspoken words to balance the clues.

Catching up with each other halfway to where we're going
any day is a possibility; and an unexpected extra.
We meet in a station, or we coincide in the bathroom,
we cross and merge in parallels less than a pillow apart:
joined-up people, finding the world as wide as our bed.

Breakfast, Palermo

One golden glazed bun, sliced open.
One scoop of custardy ice cream, speckled
with chips of fruit and chocolate.
Sandwich them lavishly.

To be eaten in uniform by a young soldier,
with one careless hand, espresso in the other.
At the chrome bar, more coffee is hissing.
Sunshine slants in early, yellow.
Not a speck on his trousers.

Mall of Mammoths

Minneapolis, 1992

They've built the Mall of America
            on a prairie near the airport:
a hangar to protect the world
            from the Minnesota climate.
The big everything – Bloomingdales
            to a blimp made of Lego:
leave the kids on flume rides and roller coasters.
            Get shopping.

Some of the shops are still discreetly unlet,
            given the recession.
One corner unit houses a sideshow
            of travelling Russians
bringing the Great Siberian Mammoths
            from that North to this,
with a support of stuffed wolverine, beaver,
            and three types of lemming.

The big attraction is
            the whole baby mammoth, who lost his mother.
Though his feet are still hairy,
            his body is now a dark brown leather
like my second-hand flying jacket
            with several additional sleeves,
laid out bulky but deflated,
            the breathing occupant missing.

Glass tanks of fluid contain
            his heart and his penis, on display:
that dead infant's plaything
            could incite grown men to envy.
Beside him, a full skeleton with twirling tusks,
            but not his mother;
and a skull – 'Yes, you may touch!'
            – its features worn down to melting.

Back at the entrance,
        three Russian women in smocks
are selling lacquerwork nesting dolls
        and fairytale boxes;
enamel mammoth brooches –
        'I Am From Siberia' – and trays
full of remaindered Lenins.
        I am in America, and buying.

Fall

for Carl Morse

This New England fall, they say, so disappointing:
the damp summer. But for novice visitors it burns enough
in yellows; in a few red hollows there's a reliable
burst of swamp maples. The dead ones are sugar maples:
something is wrong, they have been wasting.

I've just been in Manhattan. Central Park has scarcely turned,
but 'down East' maybe those rocky Maine forests are more
the true explosive colour. I'm trying to absorb
some of the American intensities. People say to me:
'I'm tired of New York' – meaning, 'Too many friends are dead.'

Over in a Chelsea brownstone, there's the glow of a hermit's cave.
He came back from Maine ten years ago, burning. His table
is spread, he chooses things for the light, the angle
of the shadow on the seventeenth floor: and still
whatever he can get said and done comes hot from within.

Once upon a time, he says, he went back to the woods: plain
furniture, his milltown background, chopping logs. Hardships
refine simplicities. There at home, he heard from the neighbours
and the local policeman. The way they saw it came down to
who wants this queer back anyway? So they brought their guns.

All along the Appalachian system, the volcanic intrusions,
the metamorphics, even in Manhattan. Central Park
shows the rocks that ancient heat and pressure made
solid enough to build New York. City of live and dead, gathered
where he can clang his bell and call his heretic psalm.

BLAIR GIBB

From Blair Gibb's diaries:

'Writing exists as a prod, a goad, a defense against the encroaching daili-
ness of middle age. With luck, it is an antidote to self-importance instead
of an expression of it.

Tom's Diner, West 112th Street, NYC

They say you should only write about death
if you're dying. In that case, I say, we'd all better
sit down and put pen to paper, toot sweet –
even though, back here at Tom's counter,
you could almost believe in the life everlasting.

Nothing seems changed since the Sundays
and Saturdays when, shins taped, I'd show up
at six-thirty, ready to balance five plates of eggs at a time,
at a trot. Lou's still here, pouring the infinite coffee cup –
except, I remember, his name then was Ralph.

Outside the door, they're queuing for lunch. Up here
Broadway isn't the Great White Way of the tours
but a wide village street, and this is the pavement
where that year a cornice stone slipped from its moorings
and dove through the head of a girl walking home.

From that height, her bright hair must have been
indistinguishable from, say, my son's, walking home
now on these streets from his night shift. I accept
that the darkness, the years, can't hide him forever
from a sky that sees everyone, everywhere –

that eternity ends at Tom's door. Lou won't give me
that bottomless cup to take home for the night:
I can't balance five plates any more. But no matter –
we're indistinguishable, you and I, from that height,
and the sky will throw anything, anywhere.

Where You Were Born

You can always borrow someone else's, but in the end
no agony compares to the one you're born with –
metals buried in your earth end up in your bone.
And I was born into the brave new world
of the Virgin Queen, Virginia, where in 1619
the first slaves arrived (the same year as, not parenthetically,
the first woman) to serve the colonists, and ever since
no one born there could be virgin. You can run,
never go back, do what you will, the blood's still in your blood.

It feels a lot like Germany – history hot around your neck.
A White can say: my family never did own slaves, join the Nazis.
His child can say: I never persecuted Blacks, the Jews.
Yet to the northerner, the Black, the Jew,
the conquered Dutch or Poles, these words don't matter,
the card is always in your pocket. They can see,
even if you lose your accent, who you are
and what you mean.

I read that the Nez Perce recently returned to north Montana
where Chief Joseph's tribe lost their last battle.
They came to try to lay to rest the souls
of women, men and children who were slaughtered there,
whose cries the old ones still can hear. They led
their appaloosas, riderless, around the killing ground,
eagle feathers flying. They say it might take years,
and many more such ceremonies, before the screaming stops.

My great-great-uncle's ceremony was to write a book. One chapter
describes a slave auction he witnessed as a child, and ends like this:
'Virginians! you who in our day were led by Lee and Jackson!
have you read this chapter? Is it true or untrue?
Ask yourselves calmly. The time has now come
when you ought to try to satisfy yourselves
wherein your old system was wrong and unjustifiable,
as well as wherein it was right.

One who loves you wrote this story:
one who was your comrade in the fight you lost;
one who has no word of blame for you . . .
it is not written when the truth can do you harm.
It is not written by an alien in feeling,
or an enthusiast for an abstract idea. It is written
to make you think – to make you ask yourselves
whether you can, before God, claim
that all was as it should be when we had slavery . . .
its abolition was a greater blessing to us
even than to the slaves, and that emancipation was worth
all we surrendered, all the precious lives destroyed;
and to bring you to confess: the time has come at last when,
through our tears, true Confederates
ought to thank God that slavery died at Appomattox.'

Believe it or not, his name was Wise, and I could tell him now:
John Wise, I am your great-great-niece, and I could lead
a thousand horses and a thousand mules, all riderless,
around this land my grandparents are buried in; the screaming
wouldn't stop. I could lead them, seagull feathers flying,
across to Liverpool, and to Port Harcourt, all of us
swimming in the bloody salt together – it wouldn't be enough.
And this is not abstraction: twenty years apart, I lay
skin to skin with one Black woman, one Black man.
We tried to scrub that history away and couldn't –
we would have had to scrape those skins off,
be someone other than we were, someone
who couldn't hear the owl in the tree, singing those deaths.

So I will pass the reins on when I die, and my son
will pass that horse's foal to his son. Wherever we were born,
whatever reins we hold, we have no choice
but to continue with the ceremony –
and hope, in some new century, to see
set free the ones we loved, and ourselves set free.

Regent's Park Sampler

After his flight across the ocean in a box,
then six months (three and a half dog-years)
in a barely larger box, this is where I brought him first.
I have a photograph: of black dog against green grass,
off in the distance – all four paws in the air,
ears and tail flying in a cry of dumb delight
at soft earth's comfort on raw skin
where the long concrete confinement
ate away his velvet coat and turned his muzzle gray.

Now, many mornings later, it's become our park.
I could close my eyes, anywhere on earth, and hear its voices:
I used to think the old man calling hoarsely, 'Charley! Charley!'
had a perpetually lost dog, until the day he told me
that Charley was a goose, who comes from the lake
to him, only to him, for food.

Then there are the operatic whoops I hear,
on quiet mornings, from my bedroom window,
a mile away – I thought they were the call
of some strange gull, until I paid my way
into the zoo, and found the slender gibbon in her cage.
So rare she once had been a sultan's,
she was kept a pet inside his palace
till she went mad and moved to London.
Now, half-free, she sees real trees above her net,
swings for them! swings for them!
– and cries, making the children laugh
the way they might laugh at all of us,
man, woman, dog, goose, ape,
trying to leap free of stone and loneliness,
swinging for the urban canopy.

Machipongo Wood

Wiregrass of trees, splurge of trees – down here
southern pine's just another crop, except
you don't have to spray it, and it's fifty years
between harvests, give or take.
Wait too long, the pine beetle gets it and it rots,
no use to anyone. You sign a contract,
the company comes with trucks and saws,
cuts, covers its tracks, and goes.
I saw the hardwoods standing alone
against the sky when I came back –
some hundred-foot-high sycamores,
a few small oaks. In the emptied space
were only bobwhites calling,
underbrush and long yellow grass swept down,
defended by flying legions of mosquitos.
I needed someone to talk to, so I said to the old man
at my side: when I was tall as this neon stickweed
you were as dense in your boots as a dirt star.
You sang in your bed, the last time
I saw you. Now you're so dispersed
I can put my hand right through you,
and the city girl who cuts my hair
says she likes the gray coming through the dark
of the grain, like wood.

We've planted $1500 worth of seedlings,
but my son will be an old man
before he walks past this wild cherry
and sees the woods that I remember.
He'll say to the fine mist of a grandfather
at his side: the time has passed
like the half-life of a mosquito.
Most ordinary of trees, the pines are down now
but a stranger who saw them once,
heads high in the wind of a storm
blown in from the Bay, says that they sang.

Baptism

We drove our various cars
southward along the shores of Hendrik Hudson's river,
then west, backs turned to the August sun.
Speeding and laughing, we climbed an hour
on hot black roads laid down
over the old ones' forgotten trails, not having
to move slowly, watch and listen the way they did.
'People of the loud footsteps,' they might have called
our wandering race, if they had still been watching.

We were four couples on that mountain, and you,
the first child, your knees and wrists still newborn-thin.
We left our cars behind the empty cabin,
tumbled across an open field and sprawled
at last around the shining pond like lambs
still innocent of autumn, believing that grass
will always grow greener, nights always warmer.
In time I picked you up, walked in with you
up to my waist. The others came after, everything
gone quiet, except for the water saying *shush*.
I don't remember what we said. You didn't mind
the gentle splashes on your head before we waded out
again, trailing wet clothes and laughter.

Oh, my son – you know better than I do by now:
how trails can be lost, love can be lost,
the waters lost, the world itself
lost – but remember when their cool clearness
ran down your new face, remember
when they all held you.

Vigil

Mammals cling so! It must come
from the breast, this never wanting to let go.
Off to the west, a wolf stands
over the snowy body of his mate. How long
does he wait? Until her spirit struggles free
and dissipates? Through how many cold moons
does a prisoner's mother lie awake and listen
for the crack of bones? As many
as the racking breaths in an upstairs bedroom,
where an old man clutches his sheet
with hands the color of gardenias
until his daughter whispers, 'You can go.'

And the small red animal inside my chest
waits only for the sun to rise and set,
and rise and set again
often enough for its own grief to be done.

SHARON MORRIS

Sharon Morris writes:

'The Purpose of Blue' is a sequence of forty sonnets that I started to write on a visit to California. I think of each poem as a snapshot, the shutter capturing a brief moment, the frame focusing attention on a particular view. I wanted each poem to hold the jewel-like quality of the image, the way a photograph intensifies colour. But that simple act of seeing is so quickly followed by other associations, feelings, thoughts and memories; holding on to what I love becomes an interrogation of experience.

I became drawn to the Petrarchan sonnet because of its structure – two quatrains and the 'turn' into two tercets – which lends itself to this shift from perception to reflection. To my surprise the first drafts of these poems seemed to be 'sonnets in waiting', with image and reflection already organised around a 'turn' and internal rhymes that suggested a rhyme scheme that would form the vertical axis of the poem. The formal limits of the iambic metre allowed my language to be colloquial and even 'throwaway'. The tradition of the lyric *I* and *you* easily carried both the dynamics of an intimate relationship and the more general *I*, the *I* who can ask metaphysical questions – what is the purpose of beauty, of love, of blue? And the open variations of rhyme in the last two stanzas of the Petrarchan sonnet – as opposed to the rhyming couplet of the English sonnet – gave me the opportunity for paradox, contradiction, enigma and humour.

As I carried on writing this sequence, it became a real challenge to avoid repeating the same devices. For example I quickly found that when I used the first quatrains to carry the perception of the image then I tended to use the final tercets to ask questions, or to contradict the emotion of the quatrains. Once I spotted this habit I could reverse that relation, open with a question, shorten the line, clash two images together, shift the image from its pictorial meaning to acting as a trope, or replace the image with dialogue. The excitement of re-drafting is the writing itself, so that in the end the real act of imagination is the play on words.

Partners

Colours thinned in the cool dawn, a playful
fog settles down over the San Andreas
Fault as if it could calm this granite mass –
so tenuously attached – that one day

will be an island. It's here in the earthquake
of 1906, that in all this placid
green, a cow fell into a crevasse,
leaving only its tail – or so they say –

but today, it's like this. Two snowy egrets
drift by, as if grateful for the still valley.
The skin above my upper lip is tense –

but there's nothing here, not even regret.
Listen. What is this sound amidst our silence?
Cows tearing grass – unexpected as ballet.

Fire

Perception is detachable, like dream.
We're driving south through Northern California,
Route One's roller-coaster from Olema
a road-movie, flowing past windows, seems

familiar – scrub, foal-ochre, softened green
punctuated by pine, blunt larch, sequoia,
smouldering . . . *no smoke without fire.*
It must be fog, air's cooled forty degrees.

Quick. I see our reflection – an illusion
like shadow – a deer ripples our vision,
arcs across the highway as if in danger.

It can't be fog. Our fears soon confirmed
we smell smoke, stop the car and phone the Rangers.
Mile down the road a sign, 'Controlled Burn'.

Buzzard and Fox

That buzzard hovering, so unperturbed
with wing-tips stretched flat out – fingering
air as if treading water – suddenly brings
sharp into focus a fox, red as a burr,

now pivot of its mapped terrain. Hurls
itself like a stone thrown from a sling.
Tracks of fox across clay are following
shadows of wings to the point of convergence.

It's how you shop, walk into any store
and within seconds find the very best
for yourself and me, or the both of us.

Driving back from San Gregorio
could have been one of Aesop's Fables; we passed
the fox dead by the roadside but no buzzard.

Sonoma Gold

Fall in Sonoma is true gold, the kind
of light so heavy that it feels corporeal.
Bunches of remnant grapes are left forlorn,
dying to raisins stretched out on the vine

like Greek dancers, finger-tips entwined.
Dry grasses knotted into tethered cords –
a gold aesthetic, that is California,
an easy life, good food, estate grown wines.

We drive up Nun's Creek, stop, looking over
The Valley of the Moon – its native name
Sonoma. Sun strikes deep, as if like love

its warmth could smelt our differences, reclaim
the fall. Taste this Chardonnay, Criola
grapes – cutting as ice – rare as white gold.

Again

First time we walked the beach at Limantour
we saw plovers dance a strange etiquette
for the ocean, a bent-billed avocet,
brown pelicans lumbering north, the estuary

a tarnished mirror. We saw a turkey
vulture – head red as carrion – as if betting
against the watchful hawk, waiting in wet
grass. Circling overhead, the northern harrier.

We counted twenty kinds of birds cleaving
to where the San Andreas slipped last – they knew
when to leave – those birds, mammals and insects.

Today the sky is a pervasive blue,
the next earthquake any time in the next
ten years. How will we know when to leave?

The Cat and the Raccoon

Easy to distract that cat, which sits
at the lintel sniffing each inch of door-frame,
while your 'Luigi' skids across the floor
seizing his rightful opportunity.

But that raccoon – the black and white striped bandit –
extrudes through cat-flap, shamelessly, to gnaw
at cardboard boxes, dip his muddy paws
in the water bowl before he eats each biscuit.

It could be an excellent disguise – for
those who just barge in, take what they need
and apparently without a conscience, leave;

but there are certain people who look homeless
in their soul, others who can't leave home,
and those who never can, cross borders.

Belonging

Hiraeth is that name for the force of longing,
which simply by its atavism disturbs
the surface gloss of the dream – this New World –
where striking gold would mean for me, belonging.

It's Easter. I sit at your table among
your friends. Cut-glasses set around the Seder
plate – roast bone and egg, salt and bitter herbs.
Our questions and our stories change to song.

Yet, alone, I watch you preparing roast
chicken with garlic, salt, lemon and thyme,
the way of your grandmother; but I'm

just caught up in the whirl of the moment,
and not the past. You're a wonderful host –
the host who lets all guests feel they're at home.

Hiraeth (Welsh): a deep longing for home.

107

Red Tub

Why watch t.v. so late, as if you dread
sleep, when we can stare at shooting stars,
showers of meteors flailing the bald retina –
my heart strapped outside my body, head

back, half out of a hot tub at the edge
of the San Andreas? My impotence, stark,
measured in light years; your back
a violet slab against the moon wedded

to sky. Chlorine irritates my skin
slackening as if I've shrunk inside.
Nothing here as red as I wanted

– not sapped towards orange but crude red
that inked the first handprints on cave walls.
Now only the after-image burns and scalds.

Blue Egg

There's so much of you I can't throw away:
those photographs, the way you laugh, your letters;
gifts, candles, bowls, the blue 'Egg of the World',
a book on building bridges, silver bracelet;

your garden with its ocean blues of the Bay.
I've bought three kinds of lavender,
tall old English, sharp French plumes with perky
hats, and sprawling Dutch – low and lazy.

Colour. That's all I want now blue – and yellow
to slake my need for sun; though I'm intent
on the inevitable 'letting go'

I'm trying to hold on to that same hue –
as if longing could be assuaged by scent
and – absurdly – made faint by feigning beauty.

Magnolia

Will I see the magnolia flower this year?
Next year then, I'll be there next year. The sight
of the magnolia candelabra, each light
a tulip on bare bark brings me close to tears.

Such beauty can't be simply a veneer.
I'm tired of deferring love – flight or fight –
you phoning me in the middle of my night
to share a celebration brings me nearer,

but I need the feast that can break my fast.
Though I still feel your fingers in my mouth
– as all of you – I want you here, now.

Your flower on my windowsill has lasted
well, its stack of seeds – teasing red lips of calyx –
await the slit of spring. They will not fail.

MARTHA KAPOS

Martha Kapos talks to the editors:

'The poem is a unique form of address. When I read poetry I feel addressed by the poem in a very direct way and that's come to define my experience of writing. I want to address the reader as intimately as I might address you in a letter. But for me this is also a strategy that allows certain other aspects of the poem that are much less direct to get across – at least I hope so.

'The form of the love poem, which is *I* addressing *you*, is fundamental to my poetry and, even if the poems aren't literally about a relationship in the real world, this form is something I use as strategy that may have some history, or go back to childhood, to the relationship with my mother, to some very early *I/you* dynamic. It's as if I'm addressing someone, calling out to somebody and, in that action of calling, there may be implied absence or loss. I like Keats's account of feeling that his own identity was absent, that he had no self, because his sense of himself had entered into other images, things, people, the other elements out of which he was going to write the poem. This resonates with me in the way that I feel about using particular images as aspects of the *I* and the *you*. So if I'm writing about the sea, for example, that introduces a whole range of references, a spectrum of words, qualities, nuances of meaning, which belong to the sea and then become available in relation to feeling or thought. The sea imagery, through the wonderful vocabulary which the sea has, is a new way of thinking about the *I* and the *you*.

'A friend once said that when he read my poems he felt that it was as if someone had blindfolded him and given him a whole set of objects to *feel* – both emotionally and physically. It's a kind of trade-off: because if you put on a blindfold, you can't take in the world through predictable ways but you're forced to do it through some other sense. Poetry has something to do with apprehending the world through some way other than ordinary language and speech.

'My background is in painting. In the studio you are surrounded with stuff. They are these wonderful places with paper and junk, things everywhere. I suppose it's that aspect of painting I long for when I'm writing. But of course with poetry you don't have that physicality: there are only words. But then, the idea of the word for the thing can almost produce that for you – if the thing can be real enough in the word. And what kinds of things? I want colour, colours in the language of the poem and fluidity of relationships, like the way paint moves, and I would want language to be able to do that. Although syntax produces very structured, very architectural elements, things that stand up, you want them somehow to lie down and *flow* – that's what I would like.'

The Pulse

If the heart is a house my parents
live there separated by a wall.

Tall rooms are secretly linked
by long muscular stairs, a pyramid

of light I travel up to the point
of their joining. If only I could see

under their door the glowing bubble
the light comes from, the quick pulse

at the centre beating like concussion:
the hidden verb of their talk.

In a lit corner of the hall
I can see their two bodies bend

apart like a river forking.
Hear their neat footsteps pause

on the turning-point of the stairs.
An exact door clicks.

Then the dark house makes
untranslated language in the night:

pound and pound, pound,
overheard from my bed.

Sun in the Kitchen

It's these freak storms.
Shining like a lunatic
your smile plays hell

with all astronomy. That cold
luminous arc, the blinding white
ellipse. Like watching a drop

of water always about to fall.
It's the door of a safe slowly
swinging closed on a million

dollar room, spectacularly lit,
a black box shut in the ground
hiding its information like a skull.

But look both ways. Flames play
over the backs of your hands.
Even as we sit faces facing,

bushes break apart and it comes
out into the open. Now it openly
conceals its blazing secret

behind a cloud. Round a bend
a brisk traveller vanishes
down a path like a broken thread.

A few words spoken with calm.
And in the weedy lost mood
of the sea I can just make out

a pale green room rising and falling
near the bottom. There are two
small people sitting at a table.

Wolf in the Kitchen

You wait crouched down behind
your eyes, so deeply out of reach
I frighten you by moving
my hand too quickly.
Funny how we can still sit
as usual in the empty kitchen after
the law of gravity has been abolished,

the table stretching between us
with the food going cold.
Motionless talk hangs
in dry particles suspended in space,
the restless knives and plates never
seem to relax, the glasses are full
of promises grown small.

And there is a wind crossing a field felt
lightly against the face.
You are a wolf stepping gingerly

from a wood. The sides of your body
panels of light, your essential tongue,
your perfect claws and teeth shut in.
A little mercury grows
brighter and brighter, your hunger rages

like a tear. Shining silently you burn
inside your unfathomable fur.
Ears abashed, eyes
round and scared. (Keep still
or you will startle him.)
You are stepping gingerly from a black
wood into a wide yellow field.

Now move slowly, move
without moving, and I am as yellow
as the field itself,
as black as the wet trees' bark,
a nothing in the air, unseen, a pause,
a different scent. Drops of saliva stick
to the hairs around your mouth.
It is my heart's desire, come
and let me feed you. I hold out my hand
like a beggar and you are released.
It is the deep red time of the body,
I offer it as meat.

Small Anti-Depressant

Clouds indolently loiter,
fitting the sea like a lid.
A stunned tongue locked

in a bell makes no more sound
than an insect's trapped banging
against the paper shade of a lamp.

It feels good to unbolt the window
to release a huge headlong bee.

The Flood

Silly even to think closing
the doors would do any good.
So when the water rose
between the tiles, we thought ok
let's put everything up on slightly
higher shelves, slip bricks under
the corners of the cooker, jack
up the legs of the table. It was then
the river grew large, began running
distractedly like a wounded dog
smelling sweetly of rain, rankly
of earth, poured over the threshold,
flooded the floor, tossing leaves,
a tennis ball of fluorescent green,
the muddled ruins of a coat,
lapped and sucked the furniture,
left foam in the closed drawers.
A pool formed in the dented
crown of a hat. The stuffed chairs became
oddly dark. We could hear it
breathing from the second floor,
a sound of dull concussion beating
quietly in an empty cupboard.

We slept close to it like a heart
at night, an eyelid covering an eye.
How did we know it would be day
inside the room and outside,
filling the corners, the sky and all
available space? Nor could we plan
the way the house would melt
and lose its form, ceilings floating
wide-open and apart, walls
sagging window-frames out of square,
nor how still the varied contents of
the house would lie in new
and strange positions looking up,
an ebb-tide pointing out a wreck,
nor afterwards, on the table,

how carefully the sun would pick
a few cups and spoons, mark
new shadows precisely on the cloth,
and speak their meticulous names:
white, silver, blue.

The Swing

A push as light as a hat.
    Pointing your accurate legs,
full length on your back you rise

on loan to the sky.
    You've gone swimming way
over your head in air. Milkweed bursts

and drifts, so much white
    bleeds from the open pod
that light as a city of cream

you've begun to grow wide, to spill
    over the rim, to branch
like the edge of a cloud.

Trees arrive and open small green fans,
    a hill bends down
behind another hill. And here

again and again above you hangs
    the world turned upside-down,
the door you enter feet first

flush with the tops of trees,
    the blue floor where you walk
on the sky. You are now so high

that down the stairs in the morning
    you find the sun,
a tiny wafer of white, is rising

from an envelope there on the mat,
    a tree trembling
behind the house dropping its bark:

two thin bare legs step through
    the narrow trunk. Hold on
to the toppling moment before it falls,

hi-lili, hi-lili, hi-lo.
     But this is the toy of here and gone,
touchwood, shadowtouch, tip and run,

for all is out
     at the end of the swing
hi-lili, hi-lili, hi-lo.

The world repeats
     its scurry away.
Don't ask me how I know.

Looking for the Heart

The small intelligent places know
where it is kept.
The cushions all tilt up
like stones disclosing squares
of bleached white grass,
a nest of cellophane,
a broken match, the body
of a moth. I slide my fingers down
inside the arm, along the back:
a paperclip, a yellow
pencil stub. Somewhere in the house
a pea is beating quietly, remotely,
under sixteen mattresses hiding
in the dark, a kiss living
in a box on top of the wardrobe.

While I rush and shine in a rage
of looking, bright as an engine
doing a thousand revolutions per minute
in neutral, blithe as a toy boat
sailing straight into a paper bag,
I'm down among the lost
long lanes, the backs of cupboards,
the overcast dusk under beds,
digging into the soft
insides of drawers, among
the unpaired socks, the hard belts;
deep in the wet weeds, my hands
encounter a snail. Yet the drawers
stick out with nothing wrong, dry
as tongues at the clinic, books lie
unpiled in ruins, shelves desolate as streets.

Now ten feet tall with a tiny head,
hollow as the Tin Woodsman, and echoing
like the spaces under a bridge,
I'm clanking down the stairs, one foot out
in front of the other, lifting each
puppet wrist in turn. I'm entering

the room as reluctantly as a party.
A door you can't argue with, a carpet
flinging a low sidelong glance.
It's either the crumpled curtains standing
by the window or the utter
silence of a chair. A smooth polished table
keeps me circling at arm's length.

JOHN HAYNES

John Haynes writes:

'Letter to Patience' is a book-length poem written in the form of a letter to the owner of a small bar in a township in Nigeria. She was formerly a leftist don who has left the university. The Letter Writer is a former colleague, now in England in the house of his dying father and unable to return. He thinks through his relation with Patience and through her, and her small bar, his relation to Nigeria. His letter jumps from one thing to another, the unity of the poem being based on the return of a theme in different settings and variations throughout the poem.

In this selection the Letter Writer thinks through his own experience of Africa in relation to inherited ideas about it. His parents' careers in summer shows were based on a music that derives from Africa and stereotypes of Africa. These stereotypes are bound up with older perceptions of sexuality and the idealisations found in fifteenth-century love poetry, in turn connected to astronomy, navigation and colonisation, connections found also in his reading of Freud, whose fascination with the primitive goes back to European folktales about transformations of men into beasts.

Astronomy, navigation and colonialism are also connected to time and place in the sense that Nigeria and Britain lie almost along the same longitude, and the grid of imaginary lines over the map reflects the geometry of the Letter Writer's public school education. The grid pattern of the township built by former public schoolboys can be seen by the rich passengers in aircraft as they look down, while the cock outside Patience's bar looks up at its god-like sun.

The rich observers look down like the gods, or members of an audience watching players who themselves act out a script that's not of their own making, yet they must *become*. They are like Europeans watching African disasters on the TV.

The theme of acting and 'theatres' is taken up in the black-faced singer and dancers in the music hall tradition, then the black-face image gets reversed in the revolutionary Black Consciousness image of the white man's soul being black, an ironic commentary on Conrad's *Heart of Darkness*, and Blake's black boy with a white soul.

Against the freedom fighter, – historical, legendary, fictive, ubiquitous – teaching the farmer to articulate his experience for himself stands the 'realistic' African military dictator, whose own TV play-acting parallels that of the white expatriate dressing up in a chimpanzee skin to scare the natives. The theme of devaluation, mockery, gesture, inarticulacy, returns in the figure of the Letter Writer's deaf-mute drinking companion, mocked by other drinkers as a baboon. He recalls the further theatrical image of Caliban, the archetypal colonial subject, who takes us back to the fifteenth-century explorers and poetry to Freud and sexuality – with which the selection began.

From **Letter to Patience**

VII

'Woman's a dark continent,' his hand
guiding a golden nib, writes Sigmund Freud,
professor of the soul. That hinterland

you have to penetrate and find your void
to people with desire, the *theatre*
(Mercator's word for map) where anthropoid

and can-can dancer grunt-whirl-laugh together
among hummingbirds, melting in time,
bristly groin to delicate suspender,

the *Empire* with red velvet seats and lime-
light and the legs and Rule Britannia bit
which are, I know, what make the paradigm

of the exotic body I inherit –
Mum in panto with high boots as Jack,
Mum singing *Bill* at Margate where I sit

and watch the spotlight in my head far back
here in the dark. Pale Pierrots. Concert party,
minstrels with white faces made up black.

A chorus girl's abstract geometry
bestrides his oceans with her fishnet thighs,
our Circumnavigator constantly

invoking his fixed stars. Which are her eyes.
They mark his longitudes whatever voo-
doo dancer takes her place in her disguise

of flesh. None of these ghosts, I know, is *you*,
Patience, swerving round chairbacks in a bar,
round tables, shoulders, swooping plate of stew

and rice and plantain in each hand, or *Star*
beers flat down, to fizz cold smoking open . . .
Although, of course, of course, of course, they are,

aren't they? And that's our depth, just as this token
of the empty English pronoun I
pronounce is the same pronoun that is spoken

to the dead, or fills a singer's cry,
or was once substituted for the name
some barque of Injun gold was guided by.

VIII

The times shown on our watches are the same.
Across the map those strangers drew a net
of pure Pythagorean lines to claim

time as their own, and hold it still, and set
the farthest places in the head at rest.
So in Hogg Robinson's you see the jet

routes on a tissue paper lampshade stressed
with latitudes and longitudes of wire
and numbered with the hours to East and West

from zero, where (almost) your cooking fire
keeps time with these computer clicks. This *now*
shrinks everything into its own empire.

So much for Einstein's boyhood dream of how
it might feel riding on a beam of light.
So much for looking at somebody's brow

to see how old they are, or at the height
the sun has curved above the roadside stand
you sit under and watch the tyre boys light

an acrid drooling rubber flame that's fanned
with *Time Life* sporting Mrs Thatcher's face,
now staring from a wheel-rim in the sand

next to the railway track. Or for the place
at which the lines will reach infinity
and meet and vanish there. A kind of grace

in that, the way it seems the ordinary
earth touches the sky exactly where
your gaze is fixed, in a tautology.

The same platonic grid of square on square
marks out the shantytown, the roofs of rust
that passengers can point at from the air

since they are white, and punctual, and trust
in calendars and charts, since they can fly.
Below, the players' bare feet in the dust

move round the pingpong table. On the sky
their ball moves like a moon going to and fro
across the propped-up books for net and, eye

and hand fixed on its cosmic little O,
they crouch and swing and lunge with chip and tock
and tick as vapour trails widen their slow

motion time like smoke across the rock
music and shoulders in a township bar
and from the wrecked Beetle outside a cock

muezzins with claws curled round a rusty spar,
'Na you don mek di blod I sing wit red,'*
through gritty air to its alarm-clock star.

[. . .]

---

* *Na you don mek di blod* . . . : It's you who made
the blood I sing with red.

XII

Here nothing seems to be quite real. The flies
move on the baby's close-up cheek. The goals
burst from the faces of the fans. The eyes

of lemurs peer into our rooms like souls
beyond the screen. Now it's clown's noses on,
and bring the damned relief, and camera holes

right through the middles of their eyes. No non-
sense practicality, no nonsense food,
not conquest now. The conquerors have gone.

Into the very map's exactitude.
Earth measurers. And I can still now see
the chalk lines on a prepschool board, too crude,

I learnt, to touch the true geometry
which has no magnitude and cannot lie
and is, thought Socrates, pure memory.

It's there before Mum's washing line, the sky,
the grass, the scent of wallflowers. A home-
sickness as empty as the pronoun *I*.

XIII

Darkies, he made a living from. Jerome
Kern's, Gershwin's, Irving Berlin's. Mum as Bess
on stage. But now this actual wooden comb.

He stares at it like someone in a *Guess
The Object* panel game. 'It's from last night,
okay, when Afi brought Lara to dress

her hair, and watch *Showboat* with you? With white
beads, thread and so on?' '*Comb!?*' He can't recall
of course, suddenly frightened and the light

snapped on. *'African* comb.' 'I di'n't call.'
'You did.' *'Did* I?' And then again, 'Wha's this?
Wha's this doin' here?' Rewind. Rewind. Paul

Robeson's at the ropes singing the *dis*
and *dem* kind Darkie lyrics which his white
song makers wanted in that bass of his.

As if the ancestor within just might
be conjured up before the camera crew,
translated into technicolour light

by empathy and bulbs and cable. Through
which Kern himself was trying to understand
his own Old River Jordan Time, a Jew

out of the pogroms of that Russian Band
Leader[*] the wind-up ragtime phonogram
transformed from Czar to minstrel on the sand

at Cliftonville. There's Dad, black as the jam
jar golly wid de white lips at de keys.
COME ON AND HEAR! DE BESTEST BAND DAT AM!

When I was four maybe, his harmonies,
her voice downstairs rehearsing, and the song
like pins and needles in the floor would ease

me into sleep. And nothing of the wrong
that drove those Tin Pan Alley pioneers,
to Uncle Sam, to be safe there, belong

as belong could. Their tunes translated fears
I couldn't start to share into this thing
the tunes call love. When Mum did *Bill* real tears

---

[*] Russian Band Leader: the reference is to *Alexander's Ragtime Band*
by Irving Berlin, the Alexander being, in part, Czar Alexander

would balance on her eyes. I watch her sing
as if to me, or hear a top note climb
out of the theatre roof towards a string

of bulbs above a carpark mesh where I'm
still waiting among coloured puddles. Julie's*
song of common love and someone's crime

left in her blood. But what you cannot see's
one trace on Mum's (or Ava Gardner's) skin.
Nor on Dad's hands holding those harmonies

that Fats's bakelite *Ain't Misbehavin'*
fingers really hold. Maestro. Mastah.
'What's this thing doin' here, John? What's it doin' . . . ?'

[. . .]

XV

Black Consciousness. *The Whiteman's soul is black.*
The shadow of his body is more native
to the Earth than he is, and treks back

through myths, through dreams to find that primitive
interior where just this fate was set
and there again that twin's exposed to live

or die, that *abiku*† he's never met
who lives among the magic beasts in place
of him who'll teach him how he must forget

what I have conned by heart among a race
for whom the soul is like a clock and wheel
enmeshed in wheel whirls round behind the face

---

* Julie: mixed race character in the film version of *Showboat*,
played by Ava Gardner

† *Abiku*: in Yoruba mythology a child who dies soon after being
born and then returns to the womb to be born again later

and measures what it cannot reach or feel,
my Greenwich line, my longitude zero,
the centre of my globe, my common weal . . .

'Mistah John – he black!' Still Mbulelo*
grins across the tumblers out of nineteen
seventy-six, our child of Soweto

come home from exiled home to your shebeen
to hold our seven o'clock Booze Seminar
or eight-thirty-ish, or ten fifteen . . .

African time, Black Consciousness, 'The star
on Che's beret,' he starts, 'there on the wall
above us, those blank grids of calendar. . . .'

XVI

A myth of hope. A camouflage. The call
of hoopoes came out of his lips. The stream
was him, so was the tick and tocking fall

of rain. He was the leaves, the inner seam
of sun and chlorophyll from which his eye
evolved, his variation on a theme.

Someone had seen him in the market, buy-
ing fish. Someone had seen him in the taxi
park, holding a bag, sunshades, tie-dye,

boot slamming, shouting touts, the dust. A tree,
a rag, a blackboard in the village. *Loot,*
spell it, spell *loot*, spell *looter*, feel them, see

---

* Mbulelo, Child of Soweto: Mbulelo Mzamani, South
African writer, author of *The Children of Soweto* which records
experience of the 1976 schoolchildren's demonstrations against
the enforced use of Afrikaans in schools.

the shape of them, the words, the rhymes, spell *shoot*,
like gizo–gizo★ making loops unreel
out of his body. Write it: *rifle, boot,*

relocation. What else? It's you, the real.
It comes of saying it out. *You are,*
it is, they're doing this, say it, *they steal,*

the dam makers, Barclays: com-pra-
dor. Write it down. His shadow slips between
our chair-backs in a mud-walled township bar.

Or is it his? The girl's thighs gently seem
to swell under the table next to him.
She holds his simple blood. She holds the stream,

the leaves and twigs like camouflage denim,
the chlorophyll, the Ancestors who call
out jokes across a brilliance where they swim . . .

XVII

'An endless sense of love . . .'.† And now, yes, all
that he, Cabral, Fanon and others said
sounds unrealistic as the clichés fall

from *manjar janar's*‡ patriotic head
that fills the colour tv screen up. Same
speech, same coup, same uniform, same dead,

★ *Gizo-gizo*: Hausa: 'Spider', trickster figure in traditional fables
† *An endless sense of love*: Che Guevara on the qualities needed in
a revolutionary
‡ *Manja janar*: Hausa form of 'major general'

same mosques, same churches going up in flame,
same throats being cut like goats in Samaru,*
same *Go home!* half a lifetime since you came

and learnt the tongue you now hear cursing you.
Which *home* is that!? Each night the lamps reveal
the trickle at your temple bent to blue-

barked cooking logs, the glint of steel high-heel
tips at the wrapper's hem, the shine-black lips,
gold earrings . . . Drink by drink and meal by meal

you tread your waiting times with careful hips.
Accounts and orders, the girls' high school fees,
the licence bribes, the breakages, the tips:

as if these rituals of coping, these
seconds linked to seconds without break,
answered the killing like a timeless frieze.

[. . .]

XXXIII

The chimpanzee skin had been there for years,
before JD had it dry-cleaned, a zip
put in the back, some stiffening in the ears,

and took the glass eyes out so he could slip
his own head in the chimp's and also see
out of the holes. And then he made a trip

as dark was falling into Sabon Gari.†
People queuing at the cinema
scattered when he drew up, casually

---

* Samaru: Village in Zaria area next to Ahmadu Bello
University, Zaria, Nigeria

† Sabon Gari: township, mainly non-Hausa area

136

leaning a hairy elbow from the car
window as he checked the times. He tried
to make a pickup near a red light bar

waggling a black-nailed finger, smiling wide
with all his lovely teeth, his other palm
clumped like a sunhat on his head. The dyed

and beautiful ran screaming. A fire alarm
began. An anthropology professor
from SOAS never would forget the calm

eyes of a chimp framed in his rear-view mirror
as he slowed to turn into the flats,
and how it courteously applied its dimmer . . .

'Not like Nigerian drivers, feller, that's
for sure,' JD said when he'd told the tale.
Those were the pastoral sixties when expats

still ran things, clerks stayed at their desks, no sale
of leaked exam papers, no caving in
to so-called radicals, no stealing mail.

A fairy tale, that's what it seemed to him,
complete with tricks and supernatural fears
of beasts that hide inside a different skin.

[. . .]

XXXVIII

Malam Deaf-and-Dumb Man, Malam *Ban
da Harsa*,* Malam No-One-Makes-a-Clown,
Malam Noises, Malam Nameless-Man.

---

* *Ban da Harsa*: Hausa: 'I have no language/tongue'

Malam Not-Even-A-Word, a pronoun
even, even *You*, you who sit beside
me in the bar, you with your chatty frown

and smile, my close associate, who'll guide
a palm across the air for me to splash
Oh Mr Shaking-Hands-and-Smiling-Wide-

and-Smiling, and with your tie-pin on, and brash
throat noises trying to make the noises mean
the simple civil things like *Hello. Dash*

me Star, but which they never can, they've been
much too long colonised already, from
however deep down in your throat they seem

to come, can't be sincere and can't belong
to you, your jagged bubbles full of ARGHHH!
across the silent pages of King Kong

Monster Comic, Tarzan – Caliban . . .
And here's the nameless outer inner curse
you've never heard, you Anti-Superman,

Slave Boy strong as Mr Universe
who bellows out his paper agony
like primal self-expression in a verse . . .

The drinkers jerk their chins up at him very
courteously with, 'Hi red-arse'd baboon!
And how your mamma, now? How her wet fanny?'

Reggae comes up through your sandals, and soon,
since without hearing what they say you know
and turn away and dance, the beat and tune

fill up your shins and thighs, and every hollow
of your bones. And it's the skeleton they say
that knows best how to dance, the skull and no

one else that truly hears the beat, and may-
be yes somewhere there could exist that other
island dialect somehow in the way

the bark, squiggling ponds might somehow utter
some reply. How many years is it
since you've been shouting to me, Malam Mummer,

with your eyebrows lifted and the lit-
up wrinkles piling up your forehead to
the hair, to fix me here, articulate

in mouthing big. A *Star?* I point to you
and then the bottle by me. Single shake
of head. Then: *Double Crown?* Another cue.

Now single nod. I can't help it. I make
the mouths although he can't lip-read, of course.
And then as happens sometimes when you take

somebody's eyes a moment into yours
and you're remembering together all
the other times, I go back to those roars

I heard first standing at the suya stall
across the street, through pepper smoky air
above the charcoal flames, and through your wall.

And through walls and through walls as if somewhere
the eyelids of a child, me as a boy
perhaps, flicked open in the dark aware

not just of windowframe, clock, mirror, toy
Messerschmitt, but heard, as he still can,
the terrifying sounds of human joy.

BIOGRAPHICAL NOTES

Peter Daniels Luczinski was a winner of the Poetry Business Competition in 1991 and 1999; his Smith/Doorstop pamphlets are *Peacock Luggage* (1992, with Moniza Alvi), *Be Prepared* (1994), and *Through the Bushes* (2000). *Blue Mice* (1999) was published as No. 10 of the Vennel Press 'Brief Pleasures' series. He has edited the anthologies *Take Any Train: a book of gay men's poetry*, and *Jugular Defences: an AIDS anthology* (with Steve Anthony), both for Oscars Press. He is one of the editors of *Poetry London* and also works as a librarian for the Quakers.

Helen Farish has had poems published in various magazines and anthologies, including *PN Review, Poetry London, London Magazine, Feminist Review, Stand, Wild Cards: The Second Virago Anthology of Writing Women* (Virago, 1999) and *The Ring of Words* (Arvon Competition anthology, 1998). In 1997 she was awarded a Hawthornden Fellowship. She lives in Oxford and is studying for a Ph.D.

Katherine Frost's poems have appeared in magazines and anthologies including *The North, Poetry London, Poetry Review, The Rialto, Jugular Defences, Wild Cards: The Second Virago Anthology of Writing Women* (Virago, 1999) and *Scanning the Century: The Penguin Book of the 20th Century in Poetry* (Viking/The Poetry Society, 1999). She was winner of the 1994 Poetry Business Competition and her first collection *The Sixth Channel* (1995) is published by Smith/Doorstop.

Blair Gibb was born in Virginia, USA, and came to London in 1994, where she worked for Amnesty International. Her poems were published in magazines and anthologies, including *Poetry London*, and a pamphlet collection, *Tom's Diner*, was brought out by The Poetry School as a tribute after her death in 1999.

John Haynes spent most of his working life as a lecturer in English language and African literature at Ahmadu Bello University, Zaria, Nigeria. He has published poems in *TLS, London Magazine, Stand, Critical Quarterly, The Rialto*. He was a National Poetry Competition prizewinner in 1993. A canto from *Letter to Patience*, not included here, is forthcoming in *Agenda*.

Martha Kapos was born in America, read Classics at Harvard, then came to London to study painting and art history at Chelsea College of Art where she now teaches. In 1989 the Many Press published her pamphlet *The Boy under the Water*. She won a Hawthornden Fellowship in 1994 and was shortlisted for the Geoffrey Dearmer Prize in 2000.

Kate Ling was born in Dundonald, Northern Ireland in 1964. In 1999 she took part in the London Arts Board Mentoring Scheme for Writers. Her poems have appeared in many magazines including *Ambit, The Wide Skirt* and *Envoi* and were included in the Poetry Business Anthology *Riding Pillion*. In 1999 she won the Blue Nose Poet of the Year Competition with her poem 'Before Ripening'.

Sharon Morris trained as a visual artist and has exhibited artworks that incorporate photography, video and the spoken word. She teaches at the Slade School of Fine Art where she is also writing a Ph.D. on self-reference and has published essays on psychoanalysis and feminism, the artist Claude Cahun, and the poet H.D. Her poems have appeared in *Agenda, Other Poetry, Envoi, Coil* and *Her Mind's Eye*.

Roger Moulson was born in 1945 and brought up in West Yorkshire. He read Classics at Oxford. He has been a postman, supermarket manager, a sales forecaster, sold sweets and radios, and taught English in southern Sudan and London. He is now a tax inspector, married and lives in Watford. He took part in the 1999 London Arts Board Mentoring Scheme for Writers and his poems have been published in magazines and anthologies.

Greta Stoddart's poems have been published in *Poetry Review, The North, TLS, Poetry London, Independent on Sunday* and *Verse* (US). She has won several prizes including first prize in the 1998 Exeter Poetry Competition and second prize in the 1998 TLS/Blackwells Poetry Competition. Her work was included in the anthology *Paradise for Sale*, edited by Selima Hill. In 1999 she was awarded a Hawthornden Fellowship and in 2000 shortlisted for the Geoffrey Dearmer Prize.

Scott Verner wrestled alligators for a living in Florida and later organised poetry readings in Philadelphia. He is Reviews Editor of *Poetry London* and a Trustee of Survivors' Poetry. His poems were included in *Beyond Bedlam*, edited by Ken Smith and Matthew Sweeney (Anvil, 1997).

ACKNOWLEDGEMENTS

Peter Daniels Luczinski: 'Up' in *Thumbscrew*; 'Policeman, Stoke Newington' in *Southfields*, Poetry on the Buses and *N16*; 'Liverpool St' in *Gay Love Poetry*, ed. Neil Powell (Robinson); 'Breakfast, Palermo' in *James White Review, Of Eros and of Dust*, ed. Steve Anthony (Oscars Press) and *Be Prepared* (Smith/Doorstop); 'Mall of Mammoths' in *Through the Bushes* (Smith/Doorstop); 'Fall' in *Poetry London* and *Be Prepared* (Smith/Doorstop).

Helen Farish: The Contentment of the Lute Maker' in *Acumen*; 'Clytaemnestra and Agamemnon' in *The Honest Ulsterman*; 'Kingfisher' in *Cyphers*; 'Anne Boleyn' in *The Ring of Words* (1998 Arvon Competition Anthology); 'Whoever Drops Me' in *PN Review*; 'Angela di Foligno' in *Boomerang*.

Katherine Frost: 'Serpentes of the Order Squamata' under the title 'Fortunate Episodes' in *Wild Cards: The Second Virago Anthology of Writing Women*, eds Badenoch, Hannan, Little and Taylor (Virago Press, 1999)' 'The Snakekeeper' in *Rialto*.

Blair Gibb: 'Where You Were Born' and 'Regent's Park Sampler' in *Poetry London*: 'Tom's Diner, West 112th Street, NYC', 'Machipongo Wood', 'Baptism', 'Vigil' in *Tom's Diner*.

John Haynes: Cantos from 'Letter to Patience' in earlier versions in *Ambit, Chalk White Face* (White Adder Press), *Critical Quarterly* and *London Magazine*.

Martha Kapos: 'The Pulse' in *Tabla*; 'Sun in the Kitchen' in *Thumbscrew*; 'Wolf in the Kitchen' in *Agenda*; 'Small Anti-Depressant' in *Navis*; 'The Flood' in *The Exeter Prize Anthology*; 'The Swing' in *Poetry London*; 'Looking for the Heart' in *Rialto*. Acknowledgements are due to the Research Committee of the Chelsea College of Art and Design for their assistance.

Kate Ling: 'Before Ripening' in *Before Ripening*, Winners' Anthology of the Blue Nose Poet of the Year Competition 1999; 'Thirteen' and 'Trigonometry' in *Envoi*.

Roger Moulson: 'Field Guide to the Birds of Britain and Europe' won the 1996 Worcester Festival Competition.

Greta Stoddart: 'The Fitter' in *Times Literary Supplement*; 'Allies' and 'Dungeness' in *Poetry Review*; 'Initiation' in *Poetry London*; 'A Hundred Sheep in a Green Field' in *Independent on Sunday* and 'The Night We Stole a Full-Length Mirror' in *The North*.

Scott Verner: 'The Sound of My Head' and 'Her Large Smile' in *Beyond Bedlam*, eds. Ken Smith and Matthew Sweeney (Anvil, 1997); 'A Lick of Mortality' in *Poetry London*.